"Susy Flory not only takes us on a his courageous women from Mary Magdalene to Rosie the Riveter, she also inspires us with practical actions that will transform our own lives and change our futures. Read the book for entertainment. Emulate it to change the world."

—JENNIFER SCHUCHMANN, coauthor of *Your Unforgettable Life* (Beacon Hill) and *Six Prayers God Always Answers*

"This book inspired me with well-told stories of courageous women who changed the world and challenged me to do the same. Susy Flory's own brave stories of how she's followed in the footsteps of these great women make this much more than mere biography. I highly recommend this book."

—KERI WYATT KENT, author of *Breathe: Creating Space for God in a Hectic Life*

"Susy gives us a wonderful synopsis of the lives of nine amazing women and the tools needed to put those lessons into practice in our own lives. She weaves her own practical experiences into the story and challenges us to be creative and find ways to make a difference in today's world. A challenging and inspiring read, good for both individual and group study."

—BETTY SOUTHARD, speaker and author of *The Mentor Quest, Come As You Are, The Grandmother Book,* and *Spiritual Director*

"What an amazing book. With equal parts inspiration and application, this is a must-read manual for any woman who wants to trade her ordinary life for one that is God-breathed and extra-ordinary. After reading this, I want to go feed the poor, climb a mountain, and maybe even clean out a closet or two."

—KATHI LIPP, national speaker and author of *The Husband Project*

"This is a great book! With her unique style and warm-hearted stories, Susy brings nine courageous women to life and gives practical suggestions on how we, too, can make a difference in the lives of others today. I highly recommend this book to those who wish to be encouraged—and to those who wish to become encouragers to others."

—DENISE GEORGE, author of 24 books, including: *What Pastors Wish Church Members Knew* (Zondervan, 2009) and *The Secret Holocaust Diaries— The Untold Story of Nonna Bannister* (Tyndale, 2009)

"I loved the vulnerability and step-by-step accessibility of this book. Susy Flory brings the unapproachable saints and heroes of the past closer, linking them to us as sisters, helping us follow their path. Let *So Long, Status Quo* show you how to become a modern day Perpetua, Harriet Tubman, Mother Teresa, or Jane Austen."

—JONALYN GRACE FINCHER, apologist and author of *Ruby Slippers: How the Soul of a Woman Brings Her Home* (Zondervan, 2007)

"A powerful book that challenges readers of all ages to get off the couch and give of themselves in ways they never thought they could."

—LYNN BOWEN WALKER, author of *Queen of the Castle: 52 Weeks of Encouragement for the Uninspired, Domestically Challenged or Just Plain Tired* Homemaker

"Susy Flory captures the essence of authentic Christianity. By weaving the true accounts of inspiring women from the annals of history with her own personal struggles to live a life that is both passionate and purposeful, Susy challenges us to leave our comfort zones and enter the caring zone of selfless living. As an avid student of biography, Susy makes us feel as if we are walking side-by-side with these women, learning the hows and whys of their personal choices, passionate pursuits, and God-given mandates to make a difference in the world. *So Long, Status Quo* is a love message that needs to be heard. It needs to be read. It needs to be sent out."

—JANELL RARDON, author of *Rock-Solid Families: Transforming an Ordinary Home into a Fortress of Faith*

So Long, Status Quo

What I Learned from Women Who Changed the World

Susy Flory

BEACON HILL PRESS
OF KANSAS CITY

ISBN 978-0-8341-2438-7

Printed in the
United States of America

Cover Design: Lindsey McCormack
Internal Design: Sharon Page

Library of Congress Cataloging-in-Publication Data

Flory, Susy, 1965-
    So long, status quo : what I learned from women who changed the world / Susy Flory.
        p. cm.
    Includes bibliographical references.
    ISBN 978-0-8341-2438-7 (pbk.)
    1. Christian women—Religious life. 2. Self-actualization (Psychology)—Religious aspects—Christianity. 3. Sex role—Religious aspects—Christianity. I. Title.

    BV4527.F595 2009
    248.8'43—dc22

                                                            2008044368

10 9 8 7 6 5 4 3 2 1

*For the amazing women in my family
who have changed my world by showing me how to love
God with all my heart, soul, mind, and strength.*

CONTENTS

FOREWORD

You are in for a treat as you read about the fascinating women Susy Flory presents in the following pages. When I met Susy a few years ago, she impressed me as being like the women she writes about—women of action and courage. Like many of us, she was distressed by the number of people who read *The Da Vinci Code* and believed it to be true. So Susy decided to do something about it and, with Gini Monroe, wrote *Fear Not Da Vinci*, challenging the supposed veracity of Dan Brown's book.

Some of the women Susy writes about in this current book are also my personal heroes. One of them, Mother Teresa, I actually met some years ago. When I told Mother Teresa how much I admired her work, she immediately said, "Come and join us." Although I didn't join the Missionaries of Charity in Calcutta, I was struck by the simplicity and practicality of Mother Teresa's invitation. She didn't want to be admired. She wanted help in ministering to the poor, sick, and downtrodden.

Susy Flory has created portraits of nine inspiring women, but she doesn't just ask us to admire them. Instead, she invites us to join them in getting God's work done in the world. In a series of engaging chapters, she raises the question of whether our values are really shaped by our faith or if we've defaulted to the values of our culture. But Susy doesn't leave us with a vague sense of guilt. Instead, she offers practical suggestions for ways to make a difference. You will be intrigued, challenged, and encouraged by the stories that follow.

—Sharon Gallagher, MTS
Author of *Finding Faith*, editor of *Radix* magazine,
and associate director of New College Berkeley

ACKNOWLEDGMENTS

More than ever, I'm learning a book is a team effort. A huge thank you to Chip MacGregor, agent extraordinaire, for spurring me on to brainstorm this idea and then encouraging me to bring it to life.

I'm grateful for my editor, Judi Perry, and for the team at Beacon Hill Press of Kansas City. Everything they do is marked by excellence.

I so appreciate my writers' group. Thank you, Margaret, Gini, Gayle, Ina, Cristina, and Rena, for your encouragement, prayers, and ideas. Jon Drury, I've learned so much from you about writing and ministry, and I truly love the Redwood Chapel Writers Seminar. Tracy Teyler, you're the best balcony person in the world; our Scrabble games helped me make it through deadline time. Jerry and Alice Flory, dearest Mom, Vivian Bartolomei, Diane Korsten, Joe and Anita Santos, my sister Sara, and Mark Teyler, thanks for your prayers—they kept me going. Mike and Diane Dorn, thanks for allowing me into the shop; you're true craftsmen. Alan Maclean, it was a treat to watch you work. Harry and Juliana Orozco, you're changing the world. Darryl Wright, I wouldn't have survived Cuba without you; thanks for teaching me how to shift the load on the road. Dear Sharon Gallagher, thanks for helping to inspire this book with your NCB workshop. Kathi Lipp, I'm nominating you for coach of the year. To all of my friends and encouragers at Neighborhood Church, you are family and you are precious. And to Robert, Ethan, and Teddy—I don't think I can ever explain how much I appreciate you. You are gifts from God, and He is good.

INTRODUCTION

ADDICTED TO COMFORT

*I could not, at any age, be content to take my place in a
corner by the fireside and simply look on. Life was meant
to be lived. One must never, for whatever reason,
turn his back on life.*

—Eleanor Roosevelt on her 77th birthday

I love my couch. It's covered in a squishy, soft, velvety material the color of oatmeal laced with honey, and the cushions are
fat. Three big, loose pillows rest against the back, the material
woven into an exotic, vaguely Eastern pattern of impressionistic
flowers and trees in tawny gold and lapis blue. My favorite spot
in the entire house is the far end of this couch where I position
myself with two smaller pillows behind my back, and my legs
stretched out longways. I do this every day.

For a while we had an uptight couch. Bright Colonial red
with little blue-and-yellow flowers, it reminded me of the calico
dresses Melissa Gilbert wore on *Little House on the Prairie*. The
fabric was quilted in the shape of puzzle pieces, and the back
rose straight up, pierced by a row of buttons. A boxy pleated strip
of fabric ran along the bottom. It was really uncomfortable and
almost impossible to take a nap on. That couch didn't want you
sitting there very long—it was a little puritanical, wanting you up
and around, taking care of business. We sold it at a garage sale
for $20. Good riddance.

But the comfy oatmeal couch—it loves you. It calls you to sink down into comfort and stay awhile—a long while.

From the couch I can see the kitchen where my kids are grating cheese for quesadillas or searching the fridge for leftover pizza. I can look out the back window at the drooping branches of the monstrous eucalyptus tree overhanging the backyard. Or I can stare at the ceiling fan, slowly circling overhead. But really, I hardly ever look at anything but words. Books, newspapers, catalogs, magazines, letters from friends—those are the things I look at when I'm stretched out on the couch.

Sundays are my absolute favorite. After church, we eat lunch at the taqueria, then head home. The newspapers await. I don't want to waste time changing my clothes, so I head straight for the couch. News comes first, then business, travel, entertainment, and the Sunday magazine. Last are the sale papers: Target, Best Buy, Macy's.

By this time I'm sleepy, melting a bit around the edges. My head grows heavy, and I turn, curl up, and snuggle into the cushions. I fall asleep, papers crinkly around me.

A while ago my teenage son, just to aggravate me, staked a claim on the oatmeal couch. He would race home after church in his little pick-up truck and head in the door, kicking off his shoes and diving into my favorite comfy spot in one gangly flop. He made it his goal to be asleep, limbs sprawling, before I even made it inside the house. A few times I tried to extricate him, but it was useless—like trying to wrestle a wire hanger out of a tangled pile.

I decided to wait him out, so after he slept on the couch a few Sundays he gave it up. He had better things to do, usually involving his computer.

Things returned to normal—the oatmeal couch remembered the shape of my behind, and I took to snuggling into the tawny-lapis pillows once again.

It was safe, my velvety couch cave.

Just like my life.

In one of my favorite books, *A Girl Named Zippy*, Haven Kimmel writes about her mother, always on the couch with a cardboard box of books by her side. There she was, forever reading a book and waving at her children as they went back and forth, in and out of the house, busily doing whatever kids in a small Indiana town did. She stayed there, curled up on the couch, peacefully reading her books as her husband ran around who-knows-where, maybe coon hunting, gambling away his paycheck, or sleeping with the divorced woman across town. She was comfortable there. *Zippy* unexpectedly became a bestseller, and Kimmel traveled around giving talks and signing books. The one question everyone asked her was, "Did your mother ever get up off the couch?"

I don't live in Indiana—I live in a suburb of San Francisco. My kids don't run in and out of the house—they pretty much stay put. My husband is a hard working, non-gambling, faithful guy who pays the bills. And my life is pretty good. But I've lived most of it lodged safely in the corner of my couch.

My secure couch cocoon was really a picture of what I had let my life become. Lethargic, sleepy, with a love for security and for comfort, I lived for self. I avoided suffering at all costs. I didn't want to ever do anything uncomfortable. I think I was addicted to comfort.

My journey out of my couch life started years ago when I was a college student on vacation, idly looking around a gift shop. Flicking through a box full of enameled metal signs, I came across one that read "We Can Do It!" Underneath was a portrait of a woman, looking sort of like Lucille Ball in her cleaning garb, hair up in a red bandanna—glossy lips, a little pouty, with arched eyebrows and thick eyelashes. She wore a blue-collared shirt, sleeve rolled up over a flexed bicep, toned and powerful. Her eyes were wide open, focused, determined. Who was she? I hadn't a clue, but I bought the sign and installed it in a place of honor by my desk.

Later, when I was married, the mother of two small children and too busy changing diapers to sit much on the couch yet, I learned she was called Rosie the Riveter. She and six million other women who toiled in factories while their men were off fighting in World War II changed the world. Even now, as I look at the old enamel sign next to my desk, I'm haunted by the determination in the line of her jaw and the resolve in the curl of her fist. I wanted to be like her.

But the couch called. I forgot the sign; it migrated to the back of my bookcase, and I took a part time job teaching English at a private high school. My kids were in school, my husband was fighting up the corporate ladder, and with the days sometimes a blur of homework, basketball practice, and ballet class, I hoarded my couch time.

Funny, though. It wasn't satisfying. I just couldn't ever seem to get enough.

Then, one day as I was stretched out reading the Sunday paper, I saw Rosie again. It was a full-page department store ad. Across the top ran a banner: "Help end hunger." Something had changed. Rosie looked a little more glamorous than I remembered. The "can" in the "We Can Do It!" was underlined and capitalized to emphasize the can of food in her fist. I unfolded the page and examined it; it was an advertisement for National Hunger Awareness day. If you made a $5 donation to the department store, they would in return give you a 15-percent-off coupon for regular, sale, and clearance-priced merchandise. "It's our thanks to you for helping to relieve hunger in our communities," the advertisement read.

I pondered the page; something didn't quite make sense. Somehow, by partnering with Rosie to spend money at the department store, you would help to relieve hunger. Rosie and her factory worker sisters had changed the world by serving for low pay and little recognition on factory lines during a war. They had sacrificed personal comfort and convenience for a cause greater than themselves, a cause they believed in and sweated and grew calluses for. Now the department store was asking me to be like Rosie, tie up my hair, bare my biceps and leave my couch, so I could . . . *shop*? You've got to be kidding!

But my irritation that day over the hijacking of the Rosie the Riveter image piqued my curiosity. Who was Rosie? Was she a real person? Was she still alive? What would she think about the ways her image, once meant to encourage and inspire the Nazi-fighting women of World War II, had been used for merchandising? I was intrigued by her determination, and I decided to roll up my sleeves and get to the bottom of her story. So I did. And after Rosie I found eight other women—amazing women— who changed the world. I found women who, with grit and guts, made their lives add up to something much more than just a satisfying Sunday nap. And somehow, in the finding, the oatmeal couch lost its allure.

I wanted to feel alive, to experience something more deep and dangerous than my middle-class life. I wanted more than a nice car or a secure retirement. I craved something beyond Ralph Lauren suede paint or a giant glossy red Kitchen Aid mixer. I was ready to wake up from a very long nap and do something meaningful.

17

So this is the story of how, slowly, I began to get up off the couch of my boring, safe, sheltered, vanilla existence to something more real, sharper, in focus. Rosie led the way. Along came Eleanor, and Jane. Then Harriet, Elizabeth, and more. These women became mentors calling me to a different kind of life. Passionate for change, each woman sacrificed money, love, comfort, time, and ultimately self to make a difference to thousands, maybe millions of people.

Living like the women who changed the world is not easy, but it's good. It feels right. It's satisfying.

This is how I got up off the couch and tried, with much fear and trembling, to make a difference in my world. And I'll never go back.

1

JEWELRY FOR WATER

HOW I SACRIFICED MY POSSESSIONS, LIKE HARRIET TUBMAN

*I have had the applause of the crowd and the satisfaction
that comes of being approved by the multitude, while most
of what you have done has been witnessed by a few
trembling, scarred, and footsore bondmen and women,
whom you have led out of the house of bondage,
and whose heartfelt "God bless you"
has been your only reward.*

—From a letter Frederick Douglass wrote to Harriet Tubman

Last year we tried to sell our house. Before we put it on the market, the real estate lady told us we had to de-clutter. Well and good; I looked forward to the chance to get rid of the things that seem to accumulate in the nooks and crannies. To help us get started, the agent came and did a walk-through, me trailing behind with a pen and paper. She pointed to things that we needed to get out of the house; I dutifully wrote them down, room by room. The list was long.

We had about two weeks before the house opened to the public. We started by pulling stuff out of rooms, drawers, and closets. We cleaned out the attic, the space under the house, and the garage. We begged, cajoled, and threatened my mother, who lives with us, to sort through her things too.

So within 14 days we had a garage sale and got rid of a bunch of things. We rented a storage unit, the portable kind dropped off in your driveway—you fill it up, and a truck comes to take it away and store it in a giant warehouse. We gave away boxes of things to Goodwill. We put a few things on Craigslist.com. I gave some stuff to my sister. I sold some books to a secondhand store and donated a bunch of others to the church library. A local food bank took some canned food. We sent extra sporting equipment with friends on a mission trip to Mexico. Even then, we still had some stuff left over, so we put it out on the curb with a big "FREE" sign; everything was gone the next morning.

It was a lot of work, but it really felt good, kind of like taking a long hot shower and scrubbing yourself down with a washcloth after a long camping trip where the dirt has settled into the cracks on your feet. Afterward, our house looked much neater, bigger, cleaner, and more comfortable. There was less stuff to dust (not that I dust that much) and I could actually see the back of the linen closet. I was really proud of myself. I felt a little self-righteous even, as if I had it just a little more together than most messy people.

Why did we have so much stuff? I remember asking myself that question when it became obvious that the truckloads of useless detritus we had culled from the house would never be missed. All that stuff didn't make us happy. And when originally purchased, it had cost a lot of money, only a fraction of which was recovered when we discarded it.

We aren't the only ones who have too much. "Early 21st-century America is the most materially saturated society in global history," writes Jeanne Arnold, an anthropology professor at the University of California in Los Angeles, in a study of how working families use housing spaces. "It's no wonder that clutter jams so many of today's homes. Americans are bombarded with opportunities to buy."[1]

Because Americans have so much, they need somewhere to offload the surplus, so the self-storage business is booming. "The self-storage industry grew from about 289 million square feet in 1984 to nearly 2.2 billion square feet by the end of 2007, according to the Self Storage Association."[2]

I was congratulating myself on escaping my own personal bondage to our stuff, and I was still basking in the glow of my de-cluttering success, when someone e-mailed a *New York Times* editorial to me. It's called "My Days Are Numbered" by actor Rick Moranis, and it starts with this: "The average American home now has more television sets than people."[3] *Hmmm.* I did a quick tally of our TV sets: four. *Ha! We don't fit that stereotype.* I gloated and kept reading. "I have two kids. Both are away at college. I have five television sets. I have two DVR boxes, three DVD players, two VHS machines, and four stereos. I have 19 remote controls, mostly in one drawer."[4] *Gulp.* The list was starting to sound familiar, and the glow of my de-clutter was beginning to flicker.

Rick goes on to list the number of his phones, cookbooks, soy sauce packets, shoes, and CDs, and it becomes quite clear that he has a lot of stuff too. Then I had a thought: *What if I counted up my things? What if I did a sort of inventory of my own possessions? Would I be any different? Did I still, after our collective family pre-moving purge of the year before, have loads of possessions that we didn't really need?* I had to know.

So I did some counting of my own. Here's part of my list:

Post De-clutter Inventory

I have 1 husband.

We have 2 kids.

We have 8 phones.

We have 6 computers.

We have 11 remote controls (3 that work).

We have 63 knives, 62 spoons, and 79 forks.

We have 47 coffee mugs. (We use 3 a day.)

We have 30 decorative teapots. (I use one when I'm feeling particularly ladylike.)

We have 11 unused kitchen appliances, including a George Foreman grill and a Suzanne Somers deep fryer. (It's mint green.)

(Note: I'm not making this up, but while I was typing up this list, the mailman delivered another kitchen appliance. It turns out my mother had ordered a GT Xpress 101, a snack maker she saw on a TV informercial. It comes with a booklet filled with recipes like "stuffed spaghetti pies" and "sloppy Joe and egg breakfasts." I love you Mom, but no more appliances. Please.)

We have 4 dusters (rarely used).

We have 39 photo albums and 533 books.

We have 14 wicker baskets. (The longer I looked, the more I kept finding.)

We have 10 pillows on our bed.

I have 7 purses.

I have 11 lipsticks (I use 2).

I have 26 pairs of underpants, 36 pairs of socks (and 11 singles), and 25 pairs of shoes.

I have 18 human teeth in my underwear drawer (the tooth fairy stores them there, although my kids stopped losing teeth years ago).

I have 9 gold and gemstone rings (I wear 1.)

I have 3 gold bracelets and 2 gold necklaces. (I never wear them.)

I have 6 dresses, 7 skirts, 32 sweaters and jackets, 22 pairs of pants, and 77 tops. (I have nothing to wear).

When my list was finished, I began to wilt a bit. There was no longer a reason to feel so proud of de-cluttering, and it was rapidly becoming clear that I had much more than I needed. All I had to do was look at the numbers. We Americans really are wealthy compared to the rest of the world. We have too much stuff, and it was time for me to do something about it.

No one would ever accuse Harriet Tubman of having too much stuff, because she gave everything away. Writing about her is not easy. She was still living less than a hundred years ago, but the world she lived in was so different than mine that I have trouble understanding the reality of a world in which people were bought and sold like animals. Most people know she escaped slavery and became a "conductor" on the Underground Railroad. She led a large number of slaves to freedom without losing one. Most people don't know she also served in the Civil War as a Union spy, scout, and nurse. What makes these feats even more astounding is that she was physically disabled, illiterate, uneducated, and was never paid a dime for her work.

Harriet was born in Maryland in 1820, the middle child of 11. Her family lived in a one-room slave cabin behind the white owner's house. She grew up in a rough wood shack with one room, no windows, and mud packed in the gaps. Meals were usually ashcake, a mixture of cornmeal and flour cooked on an open fire. Harriet slept on a straw pallet and ran around bare-

23

foot, supervised by an elderly slave woman while her family worked in the fields.

When Harriet was six, her owner rented her out to a young couple who wanted someone cheap. She slept on the couple's kitchen floor and ate table scraps with the family dog. Her new master took her out into the woods and made her help him set muskrat traps, but the harsh conditions made her ill and she was sent home.

At seven she was rented out to a couple with a small baby. Her job was to sit up all night and rock the baby's cradle whenever he cried. The baby's mother kept a small whip on a shelf above her bed. If Harriet fell asleep and the baby cried out, the woman lashed out at her young slave with the whip. As a result, for the rest of her life Harriet's neck bore a crisscross of scars.

The experience toughened Harriet. "I prayed to God to make me strong and able to fight, and that's what I've always prayed for ever since," she said.[5]

When she was 15, Harriet tried to protect a fellow slave from a beating. An overseer threw a heavy lead weight at the fleeing boy and instead hit Harriet in the forehead. She suffered a skull fracture and fell into a coma. For the rest of her life this brain injury caused seizures, headaches, and sleeping fits. In spite of this physical disability and being just five feet tall, she earned a reputation as a hard worker. She often worked side by side with men driving oxen and was known for her physical endurance and strength.

Enslaved men and women were accustomed to hardship and abuse, but ex-slaves agreed on this: the most difficult and painful consequence of slavery was the tearing-apart of families. There was no advance warning, and slaves could be sold at a moment's notice, often to slave owners several states away. Harriet faced this nightmarish situation when she heard that two of her sisters were about to be sold to plantations in the Deep South, where conditions were notoriously bad. She began to think about escape, but she had no money, guide, or maps, and she knew the punishment for escape was severe: whipping, branding, or having your ears cropped. Just *helping* a slave escape meant years in prison.

Harriet always felt very close to God and energized by her many mystical experiences. She often talked to God "as a man talks with his friend."[6] When her owner, who had long been ill, finally died, Harriet's visions increased, and she heard voices that said, "Arise—flee for your life." So she did.

Her brothers went with her but soon chickened out. She went on alone, avoiding slave catchers on the roads by following the Choptank River on foot for 67 miles. After weeks of almost nothing to eat and hiding in thick woods or potato storage pits, she crossed the state line into Pennsylvania. For the first time in her life, Harriet stood on free soil. "I looked at my hands to see if I was the same person," she said. "There was such glory over everything. The sun came like gold through the trees."[7]

Harriet worked for a while in Philadelphia, "a stranger in a strange land."[8] She supported herself by working as a nanny, laborer, and cook. But she could not forget those she left behind, and it wasn't long before she returned to slave country as a "conductor" on the Underground Railroad, the secret network of people who helped slaves escape to freedom in the North. Over a 10-year period, she led 300 slaves to freedom, including whole families with babies. She rescued her entire family, including her two sisters and her aged parents, whom she supported for the rest of her life. The stories of Harriet's exploits began to spread. At one point a reward of $40,000 was offered for Harriet's capture, but it was never collected.

As a young girl, Harriet had a vision that birthed her nickname: she had seen a line dividing freedom from slavery. On the northern side people stood with hands stretched out in welcome, bidding her to come forward and calling her "Moses." That childhood vision was always before her as she planned her rescues. She was known for her ingenious disguises (she could appear to be an old, crippled woman), her knack for finding secure hiding places, and her sixth sense for avoiding capture. Harriet said she could sense when danger was near; if slave catchers were in the area, her heart went "flutter, flutter."[9]

There are so many miraculous stories about Harriet and her trips to freedom, but one struck me most. She was leading a group of fugitives through the countryside on a wintry cold day in March. They came to a river, and Harriet looked for a place to cross. Bridges were out of the question, as slave catchers often staked them out in hopes of catching a slave and collecting the award. Finally she found a spot where she felt God prompting her to cross. The water was icy cold, and at first the men in the group refused to wade into the water. Harriet led the way and went down into the river up to her armpits, then made her way to the other side. The group followed, frightened, and came out behind Harriet, soaking wet and freezing cold.

Harriet knew they needed shelter and a place to dry out and warm up—fast. She scouted out a small cabin with a black family who agreed to help. They welcomed the band of fleeing slaves, fed them, dried their clothes, and let them rest. Harriet wanted to give the brave rescuers something in return for their help, but she had no money and no possessions except the clothes on her back. In an act of unbelievable sacrifice, she took off several pieces of clothing and gave them to the rescuers. What strikes me most is this: Harriet was leading slaves to freedom at great personal risk, and she was not paid for her dangerous work. She gave everything she had to the cause, and when she had nothing else to give, she sacrificed her own clothing.

Here's one last story. After she finished her work on the Underground Railroad ("I never ran my train off the track and I never lost a passenger"[10] she often said), Harriet worked as an unpaid army scout, spy, and nurse for Northern forces. While an army nurse in South Carolina, she was given no resources, not even basic medical supplies to care for the dead and dying soldiers. "In the early years of the war, wounded men died on the battlefield after lying there for days, untended, in the hot sun," wrote one historian.[11] But lack of planning and lack of resources didn't stop Harriet. Every night when her work was finished, she made 50 pies, as well as a large amount of gingerbread and two casks of root beer. The next day, former slaves she had hired went out and sold the food and drink in the camps. Harriet used the proceeds to support herself and to buy the much-needed medical supplies for her patients. In addition, the ex-slaves learned useful business skills, which they would need to make their way as free men and women.

William Still, in his book *The Underground Railroad*, called her "a most ordinary specimen of humanity." Another historian wrote that "her aggressive agenda helped bring the war against slavery above ground and paved the way for its ultimate downfall and defeat."[12]

✳ ✳ ✳

Harriet changed the world by bringing freedom from dream to reality for hundreds of slaves. Trying to come up with a project to follow her lead stumped me at first; how could I ever do anything remotely like what she accomplished in her life? Learning Harriet's story made me feel, more than ever before, guilty about having so many extra possessions that I clearly didn't need.

The numbers didn't lie; they stared smugly up at me from my inventory list.

Then I found a way to live out one small aspect of Harriet's life. I was at a conference, half asleep and nursing a cup of tea. A video popped up on the huge screen above the stage. It was water, pure water, bubbling and burbling across the screen. It was clear and blue and beautiful. Then there was some music—happy, bemused, thoughtful, and yearning all at once. I began to pay attention. A new scene popped up: filthy greenish water being collected in jugs by African women and children from what looked like a weedy ditch.

Statistics were provided: Every day 25,000 people die from unsafe drinking water. Eighty percent of all sickness is attributed to unsafe water; it's the world's number-one killer. And women and children often walk up to ten miles a day to collect water. The video, from the Africa Oasis Project, requests support for a charity that drills deep wells and brings fresh, clean, drinking water to African villages where none exists.

I thought about the bottle of water in my bag, taken for granted. I looked at the pitcher of ice water on the table, also taken for granted. But I didn't have any money, so how could I help? It was then that I looked down and saw my watch, my chunky gold ring, and I remembered my inventory list. I was about to do something pretty crazy, something that my mother would not appreciate, something Harriet Tubman would have done.

At home I checked the price of gold. It was trading at more than $900 an ounce. I found a certified jeweler about 25 miles away from me who bought jewelry. Then I gathered up rings, bracelets, and necklaces and headed down to Lovelady Diamond. Owner Glenn Lovelady buzzed me in. I sat and waited for him to finish with another customer. While I waited, I wondered if I was doing the right thing. My heart began to beat hard. *What was I doing?* Many of the pieces had been gifts for special occasions. A gold nugget necklace had been created by melting down my father's college ring; he had died when I was 20. A stunning Italian gold bracelet had been a graduation gift. One of the rings had garnets, my birthstone. I began to have serious second thoughts. *Was it really worth it? Would I be sorry in the morning? Would people think I was crazy? Would my family be offended? Would anyone understand my saacrifice?*

Then I remembered Harriet giving her clothing away. I thought of Jesus, telling the rich young ruler to sell everything he had. I thought of the children from the video, filling plastic jugs with green water. And I remembered my inventory list overflowing with so many things I really didn't need nearly as much as those children need fresh water. My jewelry for fresh water; it seemed a good trade.

So I sold my jewelry to Glenn—and shortened my inventory list.

Now that I look back on it, it's simple. We have jewelry; we don't need it. They need water; they don't have it. Jewelry for water. *Thanks, Harriet.*

How You Can Help Change the World by
SACRIFICING YOUR STUFF

- **Make your own de-clutter inventory list.** You might be surprised at the numbers and by how much extra you really have.

- **Trade your jewelry for water.** Sell your jewelry, and give the proceeds to recognized charities that are drilling wells and purifying water for people in Africa. You can find Africa Oasis Project at <http://africaoasisproject.org/>. Watch the same intriguing video I watched, and hear more about this heroic effort to bring clean drinking water to Africa. Other charities working to provide fresh water include UNICEF, Sisters in Service, and MercyCorps.

- **Freecycle.** Most towns and cities have freecycle groups. The idea is to recycle possessions by giving them away to people who need what you have. Type "freecycle" into an Internet search engine, and find a group near you.

- **Have a garage sale.** Sell items from your de-clutter inventory in a neighborhood garage or yard sale. Donate the proceeds to a local women's shelter. Let customers know where the proceeds are going; they might want to add a little extra to the pot.

FAITH UNLEASHED

HOW I SHARED MY FAITH WITH PAGANS, LIKE PERPETUA

Do not be afraid. I am here with you,
and I will share in your struggle.

—A voice in Perpetua's vision

If you're anything like me, talking about your faith is as scary as crossing a gorge on a swinging bridge, taking a plane ride during a thunderstorm, or hearing a tornado warning on the emergency broadcast system.

I attended a Christian school, and every year in Bible class they taught us how to share the gospel with someone. I had a Four Spiritual Laws booklet, and we had practiced reading through it in class. I had memorized some Bible verses that outlined how to become a Christian. I had even gone through training for a massive evangelistic campaign in the 1970s called "I Found It!" which aimed to hook the curious unsaved with giant yellow billboards and millions of bumper stickers with the mysterious "I Found It!" slogan.

Yet with all of my training and preparation, I was still terrified that someone would ask me a question I couldn't answer or that I would get confused and give the Steps to Peace with God in the wrong order and send someone straight to hell. My worst nightmare came true on a graduation trip when I met Ed, a nice Jewish boy from New York who looked pretty exotic to me in his yarmulke, held in place by two bobby pins. He had a friendly smile, and one day I naively engaged him on the subject of religion.

My first question to Ed: "Do you believe the Bible is true?"

"Yes, of course."

Then the set-up question: "Then do you believe the prophets were really speaking for God?"

"I think the prophets were sharing messages they thought were from God. Yeah, sure."

I was practically rubbing my hands in glee. I had him just about where I wanted him. Time for the kill. *This is easier than I thought.*

"Well, Ed, there are over 300 Old Testament prophecies fulfilled by Jesus in the New Testament. You just can't argue with that kind of evidence."

He cocked his head and looked at me, brows raised. Paused. Then—"Well, Jews don't believe in the New Testament. Or Jesus."

What? My eyes popped open. My face grew hot. I was, in a word, flummoxed. The "I Found It!" campaign had not prepared me for this one. My evangelism confidence level plummeted to new depths, and from then on I resolved to share Christ with my actions. Period.

And then I met Gini. I had landed a teaching gig at a private school, which was kind enough to allow me to teach just part time since I had two small children at home. This meant that I was to share a classroom with another part-time teacher who turned out to be (and now that I think back on it, it's pretty fun-ny given my prejudice against it) an evangelist extraordinaire.

Gini was not only an evangelist but a dream of a high school teacher. On any given day she might be in the back of the room fixing Cup O' Noodles for a girl who forgot to bring her lunch and coincidentally needed someone to talk to. The following day she might be heating up her crepe maker to make homemade straw-berry crepes for the French class (who got them only if they could ask for them in French, of course). And then the next day she might come to class in a full-body wooly lamb costume complete with big, floppy, black ears to teach pastoral poetry to her advanced placement English class. Everyone loved her—unless you were a cheater and she caught you, but then you loved her after you con-fessed and were forgiven—and she clearly loved her students.

She also loved people who didn't yet know Jesus. Somehow in her normal, everyday errands around town, when she was shopping or taking her dog for a walk, she noticed them, really noticed them: people who needed Jesus but didn't quite know it yet. She was always telling me about Sharon, whom she met at the department store and who had so many questions about God. They had decided to meet together for coffee, and before you knew it they were doing Bible study together. Or Angela, who took care of Gini's dog when she was on vacation. She had a Catholic background but knew more about the church than about the Bible. She was hungry for truth, and Gini was having increasingly long and deep conversations with her. And Beth and Jenna and many, many more.

Gini and I both had golden retrievers who needed lots of ex-ercise, so when our schedules allowed, we took walks together on a hilly trail overlooking San Francisco Bay. That's where I really saw her in action. On one golden beautiful day, a warm breeze ruffled the grass tops and a red-tailed hawk wheeled lazily in the sky. We reached the crest of the first big hill, and I was still catching my breath when a thirty-something guy walked toward us, his black lab running ahead. While our dogs started the canine sniffing ritual, we began to chat. His name was Mark, and it seemed that Gini had talked to him a couple of times before; he knew that she was not only a teacher but a writer too.

"What are you working on?" he asked. He seemed genuinely interested. It just so happened that Gini and I were at that moment working on a book project together about *The Da Vinci Code*. We had both read it and gotten angry that some of our best friends and favorite relatives were also reading it and believing that it was all true. For us, it was an emotion-laden subject, a matter of spiritual life and death for those who were confused by its fictional claims about Christ. But you would never know this from Gini's answer.

She smiled and said "I'm working on a book about *The Da Vinci Code*." His eyes lit up, as most people's did during that time when Dan Brown's blockbuster novel was quite often the controversial subject of many an office water cooler conversation.

"I'm reading that book," he offered. His eyes sparkled. "I saw *The Last Supper* in Milan when I was there on a business trip a while back. Do you think Leonardo was really trying to use it to send a coded message?"

This is the part where I would have unleashed my superior knowledge gleaned through research and given him five cogent reasons why Leonardo was in fact not sending a message with *The Last Supper*. But Gini knew better.

"What do you think?" she answered. And they were off on a wonderful conversation, a warm and comfortable give and take as she built a relational bridge, bit by bit, to Mark's heart and spirit. Sooner or later, she would take the moment, when it presented itself, to share her own story: how she knew Jesus, in fact was friends with Jesus, and how Mark could get to know him better too. I saw, really for the first time, that it was not about pamphlets or bumper stickers, techniques or scripts, but about relationships and caring enough to listen, really listen, to someone else's heart.

I also learned it took courage, the courage to pay attention, to put self aside and to take the opportunities when they came. Courage to know that not everyone was interested, that sometimes the conversations would get so deep and challenging, like standing on the edge of a cliff, that people would back away, even run away, back to safe and familiar ground. Sometimes sharing your faith meant having your heart stomped on after you had bared it to someone.

Boy, did I have a lot to learn!

* * *

Talking about matters of faith in 21st-century America can be sometimes awkward, embarrassing, and scary. But about the worst that can happen is the potential loss of a friendship, or maybe gaining a reputation as a fanatic. Not so for early Christians, and especially for Roman citizens like Perpetua, a highborn Roman woman and Christ-follower who lived just 200 years after Jesus. For her, the stakes were much higher.

Perpetua lived in Carthage, the capital of the Roman province of Africa. She was 22 years old, the mother of an infant son, from a respectable family and highly educated. We know about Perpetua because she wrote her own story at a time when women were considered the weaker sex and for the most part were "excluded from politics, war, and law, the principal paths to authority, leadership, and greatness in Roman society."[1] A Roman woman, no matter how educated or intelligent, mostly stayed at home and fulfilled her role as wife and mother. Almost nothing is known about the personal experiences and emotions of women during this period, making Perpetua's account unique, especially as it's unfiltered by a male voice. Her story is known as the "earliest surviving writing by a Christian woman."[2]

Perpetua and Gini have much in common—both uncommonly bold about sharing their faith. The difference is that Perpetua died for it. Her story is called *The Passion of Perpetua*, and it's the account of the arrest, trial, imprisonment, and execution of a small group of Christian martyrs told in Perpetua's own words and originally written in Latin. It's called a "passion," meaning "sufferings," from the Latin word *passio*. In addition, the word "martyrdom" comes from the Greek *marturion*, meaning "bearing witness." So *The Passion of Perpetua* is the story of a martyr suffering for her faith with the intention of bearing witness, or sharing her faith, with others.

The Roman Empire at that time consisted of the entire Mediterranean world, a giant buffet of peoples, countries, and cultures with Rome's military holding it all together. Overall, Rome was fairly tolerant of local cultures, and Christianity was just one of many religions and cults throughout the Empire. Paganism, the reigning spiritual philosophy, held that the world was "full of gods who determined success in war, agriculture, business, love—virtually every aspect of life; they could make or break individuals, communities, peoples."[3] So to make the gods happy, the people made sacrifices in pagan temples, held festivals and athletic competitions in the gods' honor, and looked to the gods for help in emergencies.

The problem was that Christians refused to go along with the pagan program. So there was a generalized fear that the Christians' nonparticipation in the community's pagan rituals would endanger the community. Rome didn't have anything like a consistent policy on persecuting Christians, but when the community occasionally complained, Rome listened and acted—with deadly results.

A brand-new Christian who hadn't even been baptized yet, Perpetua, along with her friends, was turned in by unknown accusers and thrown into jail. Roman jails were notorious for their horrific conditions, more like medieval dungeons than what we think of as jails. They were often just a big hole in the ground with no light or ventilation. Guards were abusive and extorted bribes. Everyone was thrown into the same room, usually chained, and people had difficulty breathing, fell ill, and often died before they ever made it to trial. Perpetua's thoughts were not for herself, though; she instead worried about her infant son: "Worst of all, concern for my baby tormented me there . . . but then I obtained permission for my baby to stay with me in jail, and at once I was revitalized and was freed from my burdensome anxiety for him."[4]

While awaiting trial, Perpetua had three intense visions. In the first she dreamed that she climbed a ladder by first treading on a serpent's head. At the top,

> I saw a vast garden, and in the middle of it sat a tall, grey-haired man wearing the clothes of a shepherd. . . . Standing around him were many thousands of people dressed in white. He lifted his head, gazed at me, and said, "It is good that you have come, my child."[5]

After this vision about joining the martyrs already in heaven, she knew she and her friends would be sentenced to death.

Perpetua's father visited her in jail and begged her to reconsider: "My daughter, have pity on my grey hair; have pity on your father. . . . Think of your brothers; think of your mother and your aunt; think of your son, who will not be able to live without you. Stop being so stubborn. Don't you see that you are going to ruin us all?"

When the public trial was scheduled, word spread, and an immense crowd gathered to watch. Up on the platform, the small group of Christians was offered a chance for freedom; all they had to do was make a small sacrifice to the Emperor. They refused.

Perpetua records that her father was weeping aloud and threw himself at her feet. In front of the crowd, he begged her, "Perform the sacrifice! Pity your baby." I can't imagine the pressure she must have felt, as her life—and perhaps even her baby son's—hung in the balance. The crowd must have grown quiet, all ears straining to hear what came next.

Then the governor asked the definitive question: "Are you a Christian?"

"I am a Christian," Perpetua replied, unwavering, proclaiming her faith to the hostile pagan crowd.

The trial concluded, and the governor condemned and sentenced Perpetua and her friends to die by beasts in the arena. "We returned to jail cheerfully," she wrote.[6]

Perpetua had two more visions before she faced the arena. In one, she saw her long-dead brother. In the last, a man came to the gate of the jail dressed in a white robe. He brought her to the arena and said, "Do not be afraid. I am here with you, and I will share in your struggle."[7] She dreamed that she was anointed with oil like a Greek athlete, then started a death struggle with an Egyptian gladiator. She knocked him down and trampled his head.[8] She won, and her gladiator trainer the presented her with an award, kissed her, and led her toward the Gate of Life.

"I awoke. I understood then, that I was not going to fight against beasts but against the devil. And I knew that I would defeat him."[9] Perpetua knew that her fight was not against flesh and blood but against spiritual forces. And she looked forward to the battle with joy.

I wish I could end the story there and report that the governor changed his mind or that she survived the arena, but I can't. On the day of the games, the Christians marched to the arena, trembling with joy. "Perpetua followed, her face radiant and her pace calm, just like Christ's wife, like God's beloved, and the power of her gaze deflected everyone's stare."[10]

Carthage's arena was huge, 512 by 420 feet, seating 30,000 people. Perpetua and her friend, Felicity, were stripped and put into the arena nude with a heifer, a wild young female cow, to fight against. The crowd reacted negatively at the sight of the two frail women. Felicity had recently given birth, and her breasts were still dripping with milk. The women were brought out and given clothes, then put back into the arena. This time the heifer attacked and flipped Perpetua into the air, then knocked down Felicity.

The two women stood up, fixed their disheveled clothes and hair, and then stood calmly, holding hands. "This conquered the cruelty of the crowd,"[11] wrote an observer.

After the other Christians were attacked by a variety of beasts, the group, injured but still alive, was brought back into the arena to die by the sword. The gladiator who was selected to cut Perpetua's throat accidentally sliced into her collarbone instead. "Then she herself guided the trembling right hand of the inexperienced gladiator to her own throat."[12]

I'm much more cowardly and selfish than either Gini or Perpetua. I don't really have the guts to strike up conversations with strangers on a dog walk, especially about spiritual things, and I'm not sure what I would do in Perpetua's situation. Would I stand strong and admit I'm a Christian in a public trial if I knew it meant death—an ugly, gruesome, very painful death? I hope I would. I pray I would, but I don't know.

Add to all of the above that I'm not that friendly, that I'm much more comfortable in front of a computer screen than I am in person, and that it takes an effort to even say hello to people sometimes.

Once my husband signed us up for the greeter ministry at church. Every Sunday we stood by the door and welcomed people with a friendly word, a handshake, and a smile. It was so hard! After church I felt as if I had to go home and detox, not look at anyone for a while and certainly not smile.

So I don't have much raw material for God to work with. In the area of evangelism, I think I'm the poor sucker who got only the one talent instead of the five or the ten. But, inspired by Gini and Perpetua, I found out how to use that one.

It all goes back to *The Da Vinci Code* again. The novel, with more than 60 million copies in print, falsely claims that Mary Magdalene and Jesus were married, that Mary's special relationship to Christ endowed her with the true leadership of the Church, and that she carried on an ancient tradition of special feminine holiness. Brown tapped into a growing spiritual movement: goddess worship.

As Gini and I did research for our Da Vinci Code book, I was shocked as I came across thousands of Web sites devoted to goddess worship, as well as books, magazines, training camps, college courses, fairs, and membership groups, often called covens or groves. I started doing some reading on the revival of goddess worship, which originated from ancient Mesopotamian fertility cults. This very old branch of paganism has been recycled for a new generation of women who are hungry for spirituality but disenfranchised from the Church. As I began to dig deeper into this alternative spirituality, with the aim of writing and speaking about it, I began meeting people, mostly by chance, who were practicing pagans. I started a blog called "Unmasking the Goddess: A Christ Follower Looks Into Goddess Spirituality" and developed a regular readership, about half Christian, half pagan, with a lively interest in the topic.

At first it was only research for me, just gathering information. I was quite curious about what pagans believed and why. What was the attraction? I was even more intrigued as I began to discover that many of them had attended church at some point; a few even professed to being ex-Christians. How, I wondered, could someone know Jesus and then reject Him? It just didn't make sense. I wanted to get to the bottom of it, in a sort of dispassionate CSI investigative kind of way.

But then I met Chelsea (not her real name), and I realized the stakes were much higher than I had realized. She had spiky red hair, vintage cat-eye glasses, and wore a red tartan kilt and black army boots. The theatre arts director at our church had given me Chelsea's number. She had been involved in some of the productions, and the director heard that Chelsea had stopped going to church and was being drawn into Wicca. So I called Chelsea, and she agreed to meet me at Starbuck's for coffee.

I explained to her that I was doing some research for a writing project, and she agreed to answer questions about her beliefs. I was excited, like a bloodhound on a trail. I had my reporter's notebook and pen cocked and ready.

And then she opened up a vein, and I watched it flow.

There had been serious family abuse, some of it sexual, all of it horrifying. There had been legal action, even jail time. There was a financial disaster and emotional problems. The family had been blown apart. All of them were shell-shocked and trying to find their way. And in the midst of this vortex, this downward spiral, a small group of people into paganism had befriended

Chelsea and made her part of their community. They showed her love and acceptance. The theatrical side of her liked the mystery and ritual of Wicca. The female side of her felt empowered by a spirituality that worships femininity. And through it all, God felt distant to her, like an old man up high in the sky who keeps a big list of do's and don't's.

She told me a story about graduating from high school. "After I got my diploma, I prayed to God and said 'Thank you for helping me get through everything, but I don't need you anymore.' I turned my back on him and walked away. Then I prayed to the Goddess and said, 'I'm going to follow you now.'"

Chelsea looked at me with bright eyes. The coffee house buzz disappeared, and it seemed as if we were the only two people in the room. My heart pounded hard, and my eyes burned. Our casual Starbuck's conversation wasn't research anymore—it was real, flesh-and-blood real, with eternity at stake.

God, I prayed silently with all my being, *give me the words to say. Speak through me to Chelsea. God, save her. Please save her.* It was not an eloquent prayer, but it was the prayer of an evangelist.

A little later that morning, I had the chance to share my faith with Chelsea. It wasn't anything memorized, and there was no booklet or catchy slogan, just two people talking about the things that are most important to them. Her heart was wide open, and she listened carefully, then was quiet. She didn't make a decision, and I didn't get to lead her through the sinner's prayer, but I had shared my faith with her. The rest of the work is God's.

How You Can Help Change the World by
SHARING YOUR FAITH
WITH PAGANS

- **Show unconditional love**. Pagans expect Christians to be judgmental and harsh. Surprise them.
- **Ask lots of questions.** Pagans don't stick to any particular code of beliefs. They see spirituality as a buffet to pick and choose from. Ask questions so you know what they believe.
- **Listen carefully.** Through careful and active listening, you may pick up on a need that you can help with or a negative experience with the church that you can pray about.
- **Tell your own faith story.** Many pagans are somewhat familiar with the gospel; they're far more interested in *you*—what does your faith mean to you? How has God changed your life? Skip the booklets, and open up the story of your own life.

3

FAST AND FURIOUS

HOW I PRACTICED SELF-DENIAL,
LIKE MOTHER TERESA

How can you truly know the poor unless you live like them? . . . The poor in their hovels and slums are seldom offered anything, so out of respect and empathy for them, we, too, always refuse.

—Mother Teresa

I dug into my bowl of cereal and opened the newspaper. A smiling blonde woman looked out from the photo at the top. Yet another shot of Paris Hilton, this time at a gala event to promote her new fragrance, "Heiress." She looked smug.

Hilton's love affair with the media is an indication that our culture is short on self-denial and big on self-obsession. The public craving for celebrity news and photos is insatiable. Just take a look at the bunches of gossip magazines lining checkout aisles at the grocery store. We seem fascinated with those who love themselves. Drew Pinsky, a celebrity psychiatrist, has administered a narcissism test to 200 celebrities, and the results confirm what we've always suspected: Hollywood stars are obsessed with themselves.

"Narcissists generally crave attention, are overconfident of their abilities, lack empathy, and can evince erratic behavior," said Pinsky, an assistant clinical professor of psychiatry at the University of Southern California. "However, they are also well-liked, especially on first meeting, are extroverted, and perform well in public."[1] Here's socialite Paris Hilton's take on self-obsession: "The way I see it, you should live every day like it's your birthday."[2] Country music star Toby Keith agrees in the words to his hit song "I Wanna Talk About Me."

Religion is not exempt from self-obsession. Think of the New Age books and professional speakers who urge us to follow our "higher self." Deepak Chopra, the holistic Indian doctor and frequent Oprah Winfrey guest, even has a book called *The Wisdom Within*. He recommends deep, silent meditation to awaken this inner wisdom. I don't know about you, but when I look deep inside, I find a lot of confusing thoughts and feelings, many of which are downright fickle, selfish, and petty. I'm not sure I want to spend a lot of time deep within—I need fresh air.

Then there's plastic surgery and our cultural obsession with physical appearance. I found a story on a woman who has had 31 operations and spent over $100,000 on plastic surgery to look exactly like Barbie. A former farm girl from Ohio, Cindy Jackson is now a quasi-celebrity and travels the world with a guy surgically made over to look like a Ken doll. "There are so many people who are being held back by their looks," she said. "What else is more important in life?"[3]

Overall, we aren't exactly a culture familiar with the concept of self-denial. Instead, we seem obsessed with self as an object of devotion, verging on worship. It's hard to find examples of self-denial because it's just not something that comes naturally.

I finally came across an example of self-denial on a mission trip to Cuba, where I met Pastor Juan (not his real name). A tall, slender man with a gentle voice and fiery dark eyes, he was born to a well-off family with a strong military tradition. Cuba is a hard place to make a living, and military jobs place you in the elite. He entered military school as a teen with a bright future. When he was 15, he and a friend were invited to a local church service. "We went, and we saw the power of God—we saw miracles," said Juan. "We saw that the people had joy and peace. We saw God." Both boys decided to follow Jesus.

Christianity is illegal in the Cuban military, and if their conversion were discovered, they would be expelled. Every classroom had a secret informer who was employed by Cuban counter-intelligence; his job was to carry out surveillance on the students. No one knew which student was the informer, so they had to be very careful. The two young men studied the Bible in secret, grew in their faith, and matured.

Although he excelled as a student and a soldier, eventually Juan's Christianity was discovered through a picture of Jesus given to him by a friend, and he was expelled from the school, endangering his military career. His disappointed father said, "Choose the military, or choose the Church. If you choose the Church, I'll never talk to you again. Your family will never talk to you again. You will never receive any more money from me. You'll be declared unfit for the military. And you'll cease to be my son."

Juan was cut to the core at the thought of being shunned by his family. Matthew 12:50 came to mind: "Whosoever shall do the will of my Father which is in heaven, the same is my brother, and sister, and mother" (KJV). He thought, *Jesus won't reject me, even if my parents do.*

So Juan told his father, "It doesn't matter to me, because I've got thousands of brothers." By making this decision, Juan gave up his education, his future career and compensation, his inheritance, and his family. But that wasn't all.

At 24 Juan felt a call to go into full-time ministry; he traded his job making $10 a day for one making $10 a month as a pastor. When he and his new wife had a baby, there was no money, and they questioned God during days of prayer and fasting. Finally his wife said simply, "The life of a Christian is a life of suffering." They felt that God confirmed the call.

Soon they bought an old wood shack and began to renovate and expand it for a church. Juan made a promise to God that his own house would never be nicer than God's house. While the church was under construction, Juan and his little family lived in a nine-foot-wide lean-to attached to the church with only enough space for beds. The difficult conditions led to a serious illness for their infant son. "We thought he might die," Juan said. His wife became desperate and wanted to take the nicer part of the house for the family. "There are hard times," he told her, "but on God's side is always victory. Our child belongs to God. I'm not going to break my promise."

Visitors came and helped fix up the lean-to, and the baby began to recover. Within three days he was okay. "Our God has never failed us," says Juan. "We carry on under his strength." Juan had been prepared even to give up the life of his infant son.

And here's what really got me: Two weeks prior to the arrival of our mission team, Juan and his little congregation took an offering for us. When the Cuban pesos were converted, it came to ten dollars, which he presented to us with great ceremony as a gift to the people of our church. That ten dollars was the equivalent of his salary for a month. "When people give all they have, that's when God opens the doors," said Juan, his eyes afire.

* * *

Like Juan, Mother Teresa was no stranger to self-denial. Although arguably the most famous humanitarian of the 20th century, as well as the subject of international acclaim and a Nobel Peace Prize winner, she continued to live like the poor. Since her focus was on helping the poorest of the poor, she practiced self-denial on a daily basis.

Mother Teresa was born Agnes Gonxha Bojaxhiu in Skopje, Albania, now the capital of the Republic of Macedonia, in 1910. Raised Roman Catholic by a devout mother, the young Agnes knew she wanted to be a foreign missionary by the age of 12. When she was 18 she joined the Sisters of Loreto as a missionary and left for training in Ireland. She took a new name: Teresa, after a renowned saint, and never saw her mother or sister again.

Within the year she was sent to India, where she took her final vows as a nun and worked as a teacher in a convent school in eastern Calcutta. The convent was beautiful, a walled refuge from the clamor and stink of Calcutta. During her time at the convent she was quiet and gentle, a good teacher, and loved by the students. However, no one noticed her much. "The remarkable thing about Mother Teresa was that she was ordinary," said a young nun in the convent.[4]

But everything changed while Teresa was on a trip to Darjeeling for a religious retreat. On the train she experienced "a call within a call," a life-changing encounter with "the living presence of the will of God." She clearly sensed a call to "take care of the sick and the dying, the hungry, the naked, the homeless—to be God's love in action to the poorest of the poor"[5] which she understood as a command to go and live among the poor.

She immediately requested permission from the Vatican to leave the convent and begin a brand-new religious order, the

Missionaries of Charity. Instead of a nun's habit, each sister would wear a simple white sari with blue bands. All members of the new order would take typical vows of poverty, chastity, obedience, and a new one added by Teresa: service to the poor.

All Missionaries of Charity live a simple life with very few possessions. They each own three saris: one to wear, one to mend, and one to wash—by hand with a bucket. Each sister is also allowed a pair of sandals, a rosary, a small crucifix, and two pairs of underclothes. The underclothes are made of old flour sacks and have to be washed at least ten times to make the rough cloth wearable. Other possessions include a metal spoon, rimmed plate, canvas bag, and prayer book. The sisters wear no socks or stockings, even in the snow. They sleep on thin mattresses and sit on the floor of the chapel. Although her high profile brought in large donations, Mother Teresa never stopped living by the same rules as her sisters.

Another guideline Mother Teresa lived by, and expected her sisters to live by, was her refusal to accept hospitality. She felt that accepting food, drink, or other gifts from those in the slums would put an undue burden on those who were already poor, so Mother Teresa would not even accept a glass of water when she was at work in the city.

Mother Teresa's very first project in Calcutta involved inviting unschooled slum children to an outdoor school, where she taught them to read and write by using a stick to draw on the ground.

Then one day out in the city, Mother Teresa came upon a dying woman lying alone in the street. "The woman was half eaten up by rats and ants," said Mother Teresa. "I took her to the hospital, but they could do nothing for her."[6] No one would take her. The woman's plight spurred Teresa to petition the local government for a place where she could care for the dying. The

Home for the Dying was established when local Calcutta officials allowed her to use an abandoned roadhouse next to the Temple to Kali, the dark and violent Hindu goddess.

At that time, Calcutta was filled with refugees, tribal people displaced by ethnic conflicts, and many lived and died on the streets. It's a city that has always been filled with both the rich and the poor and has always been overcrowded. People who were abandoned, ill, and dying with nowhere else to go were picked up by the Missionaries of Charity and hand-carried to the Home, where they could die in peace and be tended to, fed, and cleaned by loving hands.

One visitor in later years recalled seeing Mother Teresa "personally admitting a man who lay dying on the steps outside. . . . stripped of his rags, he was one appalling wound alive with maggots. Mother sank down beside him and, with quiet efficiency, began to clean him as she talked to him caressingly in Bengali."[7]

A simple, long, whitewashed building, the home has no doors and is always open. It is still in use today, and more than 40,000 people have been carried into it. Half of these have died, surrounded by love, and half have recovered, with the sisters helping to find them jobs or homes as needed.

Mother Teresa's work expanded to include orphanages; feeding and vaccination programs; mobile clinics; homes for the disabled, lepers, and HIV/AIDS patients; and counseling programs. In all, she established 610 missions in 123 countries staffed by more than 4,000 nuns by the time of her death in 1997. While she was alive, her work was recognized with awards such as the Nobel Peace Prize, the Pope John XXIII Peace Prize, the Presidential Medal of Freedom, and the Congressional Gold Medal. Every award she was given she always accepted on behalf of the people she served, with any award money invested in the work.

Those who met her never forgot her. She was described as a very small woman with bright blue eyes, wrinkles, and a strong, determined, compassionate smile. "She is the salt of the earth mixing with the earth and enriching it," said Father Henry, an early coworker, adding "but she's an obstinate woman."[8] She *had* to be to survive and flourish in her work in Calcutta, which has been called "the Nightmare City" and "the City of Dreadful Night." Mother Teresa's work was never about herself and always about the poor. "The work is only the expression of the love we have for God," she once said. "We have to pour out our love on someone. And the people are the means of expressing our love for God."[9]

Yet Calcutta, with its many millions, presents an overwhelming task to anyone with compassion. There is no way Mother Teresa and her small band of sisters could meet the needs of all. Her answer? "We feel that what we are doing is just a drop in the ocean. But if that drop was not in the ocean, I think the ocean will be less because of that missing drop."[10]

Both Pastor Juan and Mother Teresa chose to reject self-absorption and self-obsession to focus almost exclusively on the needs of others. Self-denial became a lifestyle for them, and a way to show the love of Christ to others.

When I was trying to find some small part of Mother Teresa's life to attempt for a project, I wanted to focus on her self-denial, because I believe that it was at the core of her character. Without self-denial, there would have been no Home for the Dying or school in the slums, no Nobel Peace Prize or international missions. And I was particularly struck by her rule not to accept food or drink out in the city, effectively fasting at times. She even extended this rule and declined to participate in the celebration dinner for the Nobel Peace Prize ceremony, explaining that the money could instead be used to feed the poor.

So for my project I decided to attempt a fast, foregoing food for one full day. I say "attempt," because I have never successfully fasted, and the one time I really tried a few years ago, I lasted only until the afternoon before a warm grilled cheese sandwich did me in.

This time I was determined, though. If a little Albanian nun could do it, then so would I.

Although my church doesn't talk much about this practice, I did some research and found that fasting is mentioned throughout both the Old and New Testaments. Moses fasted for 40 days and nights while he was on the mountain with God. (See Exodus 34:28.) King David fasted to petition God to heal his very ill son. (See 2 Samuel 12:15-25.) Other biblical characters fasted to avert God's judgment or to gain His help. Isaiah described the proper reasons for fasting in Isaiah 58:6-7:

Is not this the kind of fasting I have chosen:
to loose the chains of injustice
and untie the cords of the yoke,
to set the oppressed free
and break every yoke?
Is it not to share your food with the hungry
and to provide the poor wanderer with shelter—
when you see the naked, to clothe him,
and not to turn away from your own flesh and blood?

Isaiah's fasting program sounds almost as if it's a set-the-world-straight program, a time to set aside your own wants and desires to help the poor and needy. It sounds very much like self-denial.

Even Jesus and His disciples fasted. The early Christians did too. But many modern-day Christians don't. Why? Richard Foster, author of *Celebration of Discipline: The Path to Spiritual Growth*, points to the extremism of the ascetic practices of the Middle Ages as a possible reason: "Fasting was subjected to the most rigid regulations and practiced with extreme self-mortification and flagellation. . . . Modern culture reacts strongly to these excesses and tends to confuse fasting with mortification."[11]

So even though fasting is unfamiliar to me, and even though I was afraid that I might fail again, I decided to try. I set aside one Sunday for my fast. I read up on protocol and found many different fasting methods. I also discovered doctor-supervised fasts and health fasts. I ruled out anything too extreme and decided to fast for one day, sunset to sunset. I determined not to eat anything and to drink only water or tea. I decided not to tell anyone what I was doing besides immediate family, who would notice anyway. And I would pray as often as I could. I wanted to deny myself and in the process focus on God.

Fast Day arrived, and I awoke with a sense of purpose. It felt like a holy day, and I was becoming a link in a long chain of Christians over the years. I also felt a little like a secret agent, doing something unique and special and a little weird, yet undercover. I prayed, offering my day to God and asking him to make it special.

Breakfast was ice water and a cup of green tea. It went quickly. The hustle and bustle of family getting ready for church kept me distracted from food. During my Sunday School class I eyed the donut boxes by the coffee but resisted. I chewed some gum instead. At 11:30 A.M. I felt my first hunger pangs. They were gentle, kind of like a little tap on the door. *Hello? I'm here. Did you forget me?* At noon my stomach grew a little more aggressive and began a quiet growling.

Then church was over, and it was off to lunch with the family at the taqueria. I began to wonder if maybe it was a mistake to fast on Sunday. It might have been better to fast on a quiet weekday when there was no restaurant involved.

My stomach felt empty, but the growls had stopped. I felt ever so slightly lightheaded, like a bit of helium had been pumped into my head and it was trying to float up. I held on. I tried to look at the food as something not meant for me, so I didn't feel deprived, as if it were a foreign ritual that I wasn't part of.

My husband ordered a burrito bowl. I was fine. He also ate some fresh tortilla chips with salt and just a hint of lime, dipping them into some chunky guacamole. I briefly abandoned my observer status and experienced just the tiniest hint of envy. Just in time, I drank an iced tea with lemon and felt very refreshed. I enjoyed it and savored the flavors of the tea and the lemon. Strange—they seemed more intense than I remembered.

During lunch we had great and lively conversation, more so than usual. I felt very awake, clear, and alert. I was a little surprised that so far I had not experienced a headache or weakness, both of which I had expected. I also felt energized, not cranky, which really surprised me.

Back at the house, I kept busy, and time flew. But at 3:20 P.M., for some reason I started thinking about warm, just-out-of-the-oven chocolate chip cookies. I remembered what they smelled like and tasted like. I even re-lived the sensation of melted chocolate chips on my tongue. *Weird.*

I refilled my glass with ice water a few times. Then the smell of barbecue wafted through the window. I could smell the sweetness of the barbecue sauce and the slightly bitter tang of the charcoal starter in the breeze. It was as if my senses were waking up and looking for any clues that there might be food about. It was sort of beyond my control, as though my body were on the hunt.

The dinner hour arrived, and my husband and the kids made homemade pizzas. They made two small ones for me to bake and eat after sunset, about 90 minutes away. I sat with them while they ate. It was a little harder than at lunch. I felt super-aware of the food, although I didn't feel hungry. It was more like an awareness of the tastes and the textures that I could only look at, not experience.

Dinner finished, I sat on my comfy couch and read the Sunday papers, not nearly as absorbing as my afternoon projects. My mind kept wandering, and I looked at my watch every few minutes. I only had an hour to go, but time seemed to be moving very slowly. I wondered what the pizza would taste like and how long it would take to bake. I mulled over which salad dressing I would put on my salad. I thought about how nice it would be later in the evening to make some microwave popcorn. In short, just about every thought during that last 60 minutes was about food.

I put my pizzas in the oven, timing them so they would finish just as the sun set. Then I stood in the kitchen and watched the clock move so very slowly. Finally it was time to eat. Sunset. Fast Day was over. I sat down with my food and suddenly felt a wave of joy. I had done it. I had actually finished a fast. I prayed.

Thank you, Lord, for this wonderful meal. Thank you for setting aside this special day for me to spend with you without food getting in the way. You are the creator and sustainer, and in you all things hold together. Thank you for holding me together today, and thank you for this food. Please bless it now as I eat. In Jesus' name I pray. Amen.

My meal was nothing special or fancy. It was just a simple pizza and salad, with a ripe nectarine for dessert. But I can't think of a meal I have enjoyed more. It was absolutely delicious, and I ate slowly and savored every bite. It reminded me of how good food tasted after I returned from a long backpacking trip and was used to eating starchy freeze-dried stuff. Now it felt as if every flavor and texture, even the color, had been ratcheted up in intensity. It was truly one of the best meals I had ever eaten.

When I decided to attempt a fast, I expected pain and difficulty, but I didn't anticipate the joy and enjoyment I would experience at the end. Maybe it was a little silly, trying to emulate the noble self-denial of heroes of the faith like Pastor Juan and Mother Teresa with a little one-day fast, but I feel the door cracked open a bit, as if I could get just the tiniest glimpse of the grace that God gives to those who deny themselves. It encouraged me to try it again, maybe even make it a regular practice. And perhaps self-denial will become a habit, a regular practice as a way to step out of the craziness of life for a moment and focus on the really important things. Richard Foster says that fasting helps us keep our balance in life: "How easily we begin to allow nonessentials to take precedence in our lives. How quickly we crave things we do not need until we are enslaved by them."[12] He explains that our human cravings and desires are like rivers that tend to overflow their banks; fasting helps keep them in their proper channels.

I think the secret to self-denial is that it helps us to free ourselves of too much self—it reduces self and shows it who's boss. And maybe, by self-denial, I can see beyond myself and notice who needs my help. I don't think I can ever do what Pastor Juan and Mother Teresa did, but I *can* be "a drop in the ocean." *Lord, don't let me be the missing drop.*

HOW YOU CAN HELP CHANGE THE WORLD BY
PRACTICING SELF-DENIAL

- **Try a fast**. It doesn't have to be food; try a one-day fast from television, the Internet, or sugar.
- **Forego a pricey restaurant meal.** Give to a local food bank the money you would have spent.
- **Study fasting.** Study the fasting passages in the Bible. Note the varied purposes for fasting.

4

CHILDREN IN A DUMP TRUCK

HOW I TRAVELED TO HELP CHILDREN, LIKE ELEANOR ROOSEVELT

She would rather light a candle than curse the darkness.
And her glow has warmed the world.

—Adlai Stevenson, on Eleanor Roosevelt

Once I found out something really ugly about myself at a company picnic. It happened when one of my husband's co-workers came up to chat. We stood, a little awkward, self-consciously tilting our soda cans and inspecting the nutritional information while we looked for common conversational ground.

"I heard you're going on a trip to Cuba," the man said. He was about 35 or so, his white teeth bared in something like a smile.

"Yes, we are," I answered. "I'm a little nervous, though. I've heard the accommodations can be pretty, well, primitive." My eyes rested on the gleam of gold around his neck.

"Yeah, it's a poor country. But the prices will be good. You'd better do some shopping, and don't forget the cigars. You could probably bring them back, sell them, and pay for your whole trip."

He stopped to cast an admiring glance at his girlfriend over by the cooler. She looked to be about 19. "We just got back from Mexico. Found some incredible deals." He rolled his eyes for effect. "The only bad part about it was the beggar kids. Everywhere you went there was a crowd of them following you, asking for candy or money."

Distracted, he looked down and slapped at a fly on his arm. Then his eyes narrowed, remembering. "It was really irritating. They just about ruined my trip."

I don't know if it was as much his words as the expression on his face and the coldness in his voice that struck me that day. *Could it have been contempt? For hungry children?* All I know is that I hated him and his white teeth. How could he be so selfish, so lacking in compassion?

And then, a shameful thought—I knew I could not judge him for disliking children, because *so did I.*

* * *

In the religious faith to which I belong, we don't practice confession. I'm not quite sure why—it's such a relief. Remember stealing that cookie as a child and lying about it, getting caught, not caring too much about the consequences because you felt such blessed relief now that your secret was finally out in the open? That's what I mean. And by the time you've lived for a few years, you've stolen many a cookie and embroidered whole quilts full of lies. And it feels bad.

So in the spirit of confession, I have something to admit: I really don't like children a whole lot. When I was small, I thought other kids were mainly a bother and would probably snag the biggest piece of chocolate cake before me. When my younger sister came home from the hospital, I remember wondering why her face was always red and why she screamed all the time. In school, I was mainly interested in the older kids; the younger kids were just a faceless, nameless blur of annoyance. In junior high, when most girls loved kids and tried their best to land babysitting jobs, I tried to avoid them and only consented to the arrangement when close family friends drafted me by going through my mother first. When I did babysit, I always felt more than a little irritated that I had to spend hours in the company of children unrelated to me, and especially perturbed if they were the type who looked on their babysitters as a brand-new playmate. I just wanted to be left alone to browse through their parents' magazines.

It's ironic that as an adult I ended up spending the good part of a decade as a teacher, but, of course, I landed at the high school level, where the kids look like adults, are pretty much self-sufficient, and can tolerate some teacher sarcasm and crankiness; in fact, they quite seem to like it.

Anyway, back to the confession booth. I feel a little naked putting this not-so-noble sentiment into print, because it's pretty-much culturally unacceptable. I'm wondering what my mother, my friends, *my kids* will think. Women are supposed to love children. Period. That's how God made us, right? And even worse, in a religion in which people will "know we are Christians by our love," I couldn't even seem to dredge up love for the sweetest, cutest, most innocent and helpless among us, not to mention the older, hairier, smellier, and not-so-innocent and helpless adults. What a Christian, huh?

It wasn't until I had my own child that I realized my problem: I was selfish. Oh, there are other words for it—"individualistic," "self-centered," "egocentric," or "narcissistic." A currently fashionable term is "self-empowered," and you can be sure I was always fueled by generous doses of self-esteem. But my plain-speaking Arkansas grandmother would have just called it, drawing out the syllables in her Ozark mountain twang, "pure-dee selfishness."

When my son was born I loved the idea of being a mother and having my own little baby, but I had a really hard time sacrificing my own interests to put the baby's first. Children are needy and have to be unselfishly cared for, and therein for me lay the problem. But I learned. My children taught me that my needs and wants had to sometimes be sacrificed in favor of theirs, and it was a long, hard lesson, mostly learned during endless late nights when one or the other was sick, even feverish. My closely held senses of self-empowerment and self-esteem were consumed, turned to ashes in the seat of the rocking chair as I sat up nights, holding a baby and worrying, praying, and learning to love. My baby evicted me from the center of my universe.

It was a good thing.

So I started to kind-of like kids. I treasured my own two kids and enjoyed their friends. I watched my friends' children and sometimes helped out with childcare at church. I began to pay some attention to the plight of children in the world outside my comfortable middle-class bubble and to see that most kids have a pretty rough time of it. Many have never known the comfort of a rocking chair on a feverish night or the satisfaction of a good healthful meal with seconds allowed. And for what reason? Selfishness—like mine. And so I wanted to change.

* * *

One woman who lived a very unselfish life helping children was Eleanor Roosevelt, president's wife, political activist, and great humanitarian. Often called "First Lady of the World,"[1] her efforts to improve the lives of ordinary people made her a symbol of hope throughout the world. One of the things I like most about her is that she sacrificed personal comfort to travel and see things for herself.

The first week she was in the White House, she wrote to a close friend, "I begin to think there may be ways in which I can be useful."[2] And it was true; during her very first year in the White House, she reportedly traveled 38,000 miles to visit the underprivileged of all races, creeds, and nations. The next year it was 42,000 miles. Then the reporters stopped counting.

Born in New York City in 1884, Eleanor belonged to one of the few wealthy, elite families of high society. Her mother was a wildly popular debutante, and her father was a successful businessman. "My mother was one of the most beautiful women I have ever seen," wrote Eleanor in her autobiography; Eleanor was not. She describes herself as shy and solemn, and to her embarrassment her mother used to call her "Granny" both because of her funny, "old-fashioned" ways and large, protruding front teeth. "My mother was troubled by my lack of beauty, and I knew it as a child senses these things," Eleanor said.[3]

Although born into great privilege, Eleanor had a childhood marked by loss and displacement. Her father, a womanizer and alcoholic, once left her, as a small child, standing alone for six hours outside a club while he drank. Eventually a stranger brought her home. When Eleanor was eight, her mother died of diphtheria. Afterward, Eleanor and her younger brothers were sent to live with her strict Victorian grandmother in a dreary mansion chock full of relatives and servants. One of Eleanor's brothers soon died of scarlet fever, and then her beloved father, whom she always believed would come back and retrieve her, died not long after.

I wonder if these losses made her more sensitive, more attuned to suffering. Was it "severe mercy," cultivating a compassion that in the years ahead would propel her to help untold thousands?

Her aunt groomed Eleanor into a debutante and presented her to society at the age of 18. Parties, balls, and receptions filled her time. "She wasn't a belle by any means . . . but she was an interesting talker,"[4] noted an acquaintance. Anxious to do something helpful, Eleanor joined the Junior League, working with immigrant children, and so began what she continued to do the rest of her life: to go into the poorest, roughest places on earth, do what she could to help the men, women, and children she found there, and return to report the details of what she had seen. Then, she would push for change.

On a visit to a sweatshop, where she was observing and reporting on conditions for the Consumers League, Eleanor recalled, "I was frightened to death. But this was what had been required of me, and I wanted to be useful. I entered my first sweatshop. . . . I saw little children of four or five sitting at tables until they dropped with fatigue."[5] Still in her teens, the age when I was mostly worried about my hair, makeup, and clothes, Eleanor was beginning to forge her legacy as a woman who changed the world.

When she was 19, Eleanor fell in love with her fifth cousin, Franklin Delano Roosevelt, a handsome Harvard student. They married, and Eleanor kept busy for the next decade raising their six children, trying to create the warm, loving family she never had. This task was complicated by a domineering mother-in-law who lived next door and had free access to her home and an ambitious husband with political aspirations.

But her confidence grew as she increasingly took on volunteer work during World War I. Her husband's 1921 bout with polio, resulting in paralysis, catapulted her into a political role that was unprecedented for a political wife. She kept the Roosevelt name in front of the public while Franklin was recuperating, and she never again melted into the shadows. Eleanor joined part of a growing circle of reform-minded, politically active women who worked for the end of child labor and for a 48-hour work week for women, a fair minimum wage, and the right of women to participate in trade unions.

Although he would remain paralyzed from the waist down, Franklin otherwise recovered and successfully ran for governor of New York. Eleanor continued her political activities, in addition to functioning as FDR's eyes and ears, walking where he could not walk. When she traveled around the state, she refused an official limousine and insisted on driving herself. She became known as a First Lady who cared about people's problems and tried to help, often answering letters herself or referring them to someone who could.

In 1933 she became the First Lady of the country when FDR was elected president for the first of four terms. Independent and self-effacing, as always, the president's wife refused to be surrounded by Secret Service agents when she went out. "No one's going to hurt me," she said. "I simply can't imagine being afraid of going among [Americans] as I always have, as I always shall."[6]

She began flying all over the country and amazing the White House reporters with her nonstop energy. Her personal visits, along with her newspaper columns, radio addresses, press conferences, and public lectures, made her easily the most outspoken and most high-profile First Lady ever. Eleanor began to speak out on civil rights, arguing that democracy was not complete until both poverty and prejudice were conquered: "We have poverty which enslaves and racial prejudice which does the same."[7]

Not everyone was enamored with Eleanor's groundbreaking political and social involvement. One highly placed official said, "I wish that Mrs. Roosevelt would stick to her knitting and keep out of the affairs connected with my department."[8] Radio and TV shows sometimes made fun of her high-pitched voice and her distinctive buck-toothed smile. But Eleanor could not be stopped. During World War II she traveled around the world as a goodwill ambassador, visiting the war-wounded, touring battle sites, and encouraging British women in war factories. Many of those flights were taken in a cramped, unheated bomber plane equipped as a transport, not the most luxurious means of flying for a 59-year-old president's wife. During one five-week trip, she visited 400,000 servicemen in camps, hospitals, and rest centers, losing 30 pounds in the process and arriving home physically and emotionally exhausted.

After 40 years of marriage, FDR died. Eleanor was 60. Although she is famously quoted as trying to dismiss reporters with "The story is over," Eleanor's story continued with a passion. At President Truman's request, she served on the American delegation to the newly created United Nations, never missing a meeting and earning a reputation as the hardest working and best informed member among the Americans. In 1946 she was elected chair of the United Nation's Human Rights Commission, and in 1948 she shepherded the universal Declaration of Human rights to overwhelming approval, accompanied by a standing ovation for Eleanor. "All human beings are born free and equal in dignity and rights,"[9] announced the declaration. Even if its ideals have not all been realized, CNN has stated that the declaration "paves the way for what progress has been made in human rights."[10]

As she aged, Eleanor continued her world travels, working for both political and humanitarian causes. Her philosophy, in her own words, was "If you have work to do and do it to the best of your ability, you will not have much time to think about yourself."[11] Colleagues and employees described her as warm, kind, humble, and "lacking any feeling of self-importance."[12] She summed up her accomplishments as follows: "I just did what I had to do as things came along."[13]

Eleanor died at the age of 78 in 1962 and was mourned around the world. "She lived equality, freedom, and democracy," a colleague said. "She put those ideals into flesh."[14] She never settled for secondhand reports; she always pinned up her hair, laced up those clunky shoes, and went to see things for herself.

I wanted to be like Eleanor and go someplace horrible, where people were suffering. I wanted to see for myself and try to help however I could. I wanted to pay the world back for my selfishness, to help children in need, and to try to blot out my earlier ignorance and indifference. I wanted work to do and no time to think about myself. I wanted to live out compassion. So I joined a humanitarian mission to a country with a dismal record in human rights, the most politically repressive regime in the western hemisphere: Cuba.

Before I went, the only pieces of information I had personally compiled about Cuba were these: (1) Desi Arnaz was born there, (2) Fidel Castro runs things there, and, (3) they produce famous cigars. But then, like Eleanor, I went to see for myself.

"There's the tourist Cuba and the real Cuba, and we're going to see the real Cuba," said our guide.

The real Cuba is a beautiful tropical island covered in rotting buildings and hopeless people.

Cuba is just 90 miles from the United States but eons away from our democratic freedoms and our standard of living. Cubans make an average of $15 a month. They're not allowed to relocate, travel, get an education, choose a career, or buy a house without government approval. Everyone spies on everyone else; paid informants infest the hotels, schools, restaurants, and churches. Our driver, a hard-eyed man with a thick neck, paid close attention to our conversations. He looked like a Mafia goon.

In Cuba, it's illegal to air political views, especially those involving Castro. In fact, it's illegal to use his name. Cubans call him "The Beard," but instead of uttering the words out loud, in conversations they rub their chins to evoke his name. On the streets, the people have a very stoic look, almost an expressionless mask, except for the eyes—those are curious but tense.

Although cattle are plentiful, Cubans are forbidden to eat beef, because it's reserved for "tourists." The same goes for milk for anyone over the age of seven. Health care, including surgery, is free, but for some reason Cubans are desperate for basic drugstore staples such as vitamins and painkillers. Give a Cuban a tube of toothpaste, and make his or her week. Give a Cuban kid a piece of candy, and make a friend for life.

Most Cubans have one set of clothes, little furniture, and no car. There's no rush-hour traffic. People get around by bus, bike, or on foot. I saw a few wormy-looking horses pulling little rickety carts, and a number of smoky tractors towing trailers full of tired-looking people standing, hanging on to the sides.

Except in the tourist areas, everything is in an advanced state of decay. Our hotel room in Pinar del Río, one of the rural provinces, was pockmarked with holes. Supposedly a luxurious resort, it had holes in the ceiling, holes in the walls, and holes in the shower through which little green frogs moved freely and at will. At night I closed my eyes tightly—I didn't want to see what emerged from those holes after the sun went down.

I remembered Eleanor's travels and gritted my teeth as we bounced along dusty roads, ate mystery meat stews in Cuban homes, and used holes-in-the-floor bathrooms with no running water. There was no toilet paper—my favorite bathroom provided old issues of the Communist Party newspaper for hygienic purposes.

Money is scarce, so women turn to prostitution to make ends meet. Europeans travel in droves to Cuba for the chance to indulge their fleshly appetites at bargain rates. As a result, many Cuban children have blond hair or blue eyes, their only souvenir of a forever anonymous father's cheap tropical vacation.

And it's the children, of course, who captured my heart. They lifted me outside myself, melted the facade of my indifference, made it forever after impossible to return to that selfish, narcissistic creature I once was.

The kids simply loved us. They hugged us, touched our skirts, rubbed our arms. One beautiful, dark-eyed girl with braids wove a little lace doily for me out of plastic purple cord. I cried and gave her my necklace.

A small, fuzzy-haired girl handed me her brother to hold, then asked me to take a picture of him. For what? So his image, at least, could be in America? I don't know. We did puppet shows and made crafts and sang songs. We brought small paper bags and taught them how to draw a face on the bag and make their own little puppet. I see them still, wetting the felt-tip markers on their tongues *(Why did I skimp and buy the cheap kind?)* and watching me to see if I approved, if what they were drawing was okay. One girl came up and shyly asked if she could have the clear plastic case the pens came in. The next day I saw her carrying it, proudly, as a purse. And the books—we brought some illustrated story booklets, and the children were mesmerized, holding the booklets carefully, as if they were precious and might disappear if handled too roughly.

On our last night there we did a puppet show extravaganza. We handed out books and toys and candy. We made balloon animals. We sang and showed a video and made little dolls out of yarn. Finally we were all exhausted, and it was time to go. One big gaggle of kids was from a village in the mountains, and their transportation pulled up out front. It was a massive dump truck, rusty, filthy, smoke shooting out of the exhaust. The adults helped the kids climb up into the truck bed as we watched, not quite believing what we were seeing. When the bed of the truck was full, the kids began to wave their arms, colorful balloon animals swaying above their smiling faces in the warm tropical twilight.

I knew something had happened to me inside, and I couldn't go back. Going to Cuba had awakened something, and now everything was different.

One Cuban man wrote this to us after our visit:

You have stirred up something very beautiful within me. And I give thanks to God, because I know that there are many like you in the world with your lovely ways who are helping many. . . . You do not know how much you have helped me, and I do not know if you can even imagine. What has been born in my heart has more value than all the money in the world. Forgive me for not saying all of these things personally, but I could not. Beloved brothers and sisters, I love you very much, and I will never forget you.

* * *

God is good. He shows us only small, cloudy reflections of our shortcomings, and only a little at a time so we're not completely and utterly overwhelmed with the full extent of our hideousness and ready to give it all up. It's like when you learn to read: you don't start with Shakespeare—you start with Richard Scarry's *Lowly Worm.*

So God showed me a little slice of what my pure-dee "I find children annoying" selfishness had been like when I saw it in the man at that picnic.

But at least, thanks to Eleanor, the hungry kids in Cuba hadn't ruined my trip—they *made* my trip. I had brought candy, money, baseballs, paper bag puppets, but all of it was like dropping a paltry penny in the offering plate. The need is so great. At least I went and loved and embraced and cried and smiled and touched—and I learned. There's more to this world than my life and my problems. It's dark, but there are children—in the back of a rusty dump truck, smiling and waving their balloon animals. I was there.

How You Can Help Change the World by
TRAVELING TO HELP CHILDREN

First, be on the lookout for locally organized humanitarian trips in your town, service group, or church. For your first trip, it may be easier to serve alongside friends and neighbors. Additionally, here are some respected organizations that offer international trips to help children.

Ambassadors for Children is a not-for-profit, charitable organization that provides meaningful travel experiences with global volunteer opportunities to help children in need around the world. These humanitarian trips deliver specifically requested items to the children in each destination. Some of their sustainable programs include

- Building a school in Uganda and an orphanage in India

- Supplying and shipping medical equipment to Serbia, El Salvador, Malawi, and Jordan
- Providing books and financial support for children's libraries in Nepal, Guatemala, Jordan, and Native American reservations

Global Crossroads Humanitarian Trips specialize in building and renovating orphanages and schools in developing countries. "Our humanitarian trips are very unique in terms of travel and cultural immersion. Unlike other volunteer programs, we live in rural villages (many of which have no electricity), work alongside the villagers, take outdoor showers, eat local food, explore native villages, join local cultural programs, and experience the issues and challenges of developing countries directly from the field."

Global Volunteers can use travel volunteers of all ages, regardless of skill and background. Help out short term using your skills in science, math, or English language. You can also lead arts and crafts activities or share your special talents in music or other creative arts. One of the most rewarding work projects is simply playing with and holding young children who desperately need individual attention and care.

5

LIFE, UNPLUGGED

HOW I PRACTICED DEVOTION,
LIKE MARY MAGDALENE

*Jesus' mother, his aunt, Mary the wife of Clopas, and
Mary Magdalene stood at the foot of the cross.*

—John 19:25, TM

The smell of warm coconut oil tickled my nose. A tropical breeze soothed my sun-warmed limbs as I dozed, in and out of sleep, half listening to the waves rolling across the beach behind me. We had been saving our money for a long time, and finally we were enjoying a tropical vacation with our two kids.

I wiggled my toes as I listened to the kids laughing and splashing in the pool with my husband. *I can't think of anywhere else I'd rather be right now.* I melted back into sleep.

Then a woman's voice nearby: "So what did you think about breakfast?"

The words slowly penetrated my poolside nap. *Who was talking?*

"I loved the pineapple, didn't you? It was faaabulous! Have you tried an omelet yet?"

I looked around, my eyes adjusting to the bright sunlight, and saw a woman in a floppy straw hat just a chair away. *I think*

73

she's talking to me. And we had eaten at the hotel's famous breakfast buffet this morning. Maybe we had seen each other there.

"I had one with mushrooms and cheese. Tomorrow I'm going to live dangerously and have him throw in some artichoke hearts."

That got my attention. I love artichoke hearts! I pulled myself upright and said, "That sounds great! I'm going to try that tomorrow too." I smiled—big.

She looked over at me, frowned, and quickly looked away. She adjusted an earpiece, then said, "So, Marisa, where do you want to go shopping today? I need to find some new flip flops; I lost one at the beach yesterday. The kids buried it in the sand."

Her voice trailed away as I tuned her out and scooched down in my chair with embarrassment. She was on a cell phone and hadn't been talking to me at all. It left me with an odd, empty feeling—I guess I had been excited for a moment at the chance for a friendly chat and disappointed when I realized she really wasn't interested in me at all.

The woman in the floppy hat wasn't at all unusual. Over the next few days I noticed people everywhere on cell phones, talking or texting, e-mailing or surfing the Internet. Whether we were at the pool, on the beach, or taking a stroll through the tropical landscaping, it seemed like just about every vacationer I saw was working hard to stay closely connected with those left behind.

Maybe *we* were the strange ones. My husband and I had always made it a point to unplug while on vacation. One of our favorite places to go was a campground high in the Sierra Nevada Mountains called Silver Lake, and one of the very best things about Silver Lake was that it had no cell reception. No one could reach us.

Is it just me, or does it seem that the world is growing smaller, that human beings are choosing to connect and stay connected at all times? It's getting harder and harder to untangle ourselves from the web of technology for even a few days.

And I really can understand why: social networking is addictive. One of the most popular ways of networking is Facebook, a social network of millions that I joined not long ago. It's been a great way to find friends and neighbors I had lost touch with, helps me keep an eye on the kids, and lets me play online Scrabble games with friends. I've noticed, though, that my Facebook conversations tend to be brief, lighthearted, and—okay, I'll just say it—shallow. I avoid sharing too much personal information or posting notes about struggles I'm having. I've noticed my friends do the same. So while I can use Facebook to keep track of where they're traveling or look at cute photos they post, it's not conducive to deepening relationships.

Facebook started a few years ago as a way for college students to stay in touch. When it opened to the public, it began to gain traction, and now people of all ages are signing up as members. As I write this, Facebook has 90 million active visitors[1] with adults 25 and older as the fastest growing segment.[2] Facebook is worth billions, although experts argue whether it's $15 billion or just a measly $4 billion. But the monetary value is an indicator of its increasing popularity and the powerful hold that social network sites have on their users, even while on tropical vacations.

Another hot connection point of the moment is something called Twitter, a service for friends, family, and co-workers to communicate and stay connected through the techno-exchange of quick, frequent answers to one simple question: "What are you doing?" It works like this: you plug in your update of 140 characters or less. Then Twitter sends your little blurb out to your subscription list via e-mail, text message, or the Twitter Web site. You can also have it automatically posted on your Facebook page or distributed through Really Simple Syndication

(RSS) services. Twittering, also known as micro-blogging, is another way for people to stay connected, and many users post multiple updates a day. If I had been Twittering at the pool that day on my tropical vacation, it might have looked like this: "I'm lying in the sun by the pool. I thought a woman was talking to me and she was actually on her cell phone. Embarrassing!"

Facebook and Twitter are just two of the multitudes of social networking sites, and with their popularity and the potential for huge advertising revenue, I don't doubt that young and creative minds are even now designing fun, useful, and ever more addictive social networks to launch in the days ahead.

This phenomenon kind of reminds me of the old *Star Trek: The Next Generation* television show that included an alien entity called "the Borg." It was not just an individual alien but a network of people who lived and moved seemingly independently but were actually connected by a microprocessor implant to a central computer brain that controlled their actions. My husband and I, sci-fi fans from way back, have an inside joke about this whenever we spot someone wearing a Bluetooth earpiece, blue light blinking on the side of his or her head. "Look—it's the Borg," we whisper conspiratorially. Okay, we're a little immature.

But the point is that as much fun and community as can be had by being connected through social media, there is a temptation to let priorities get mixed up. A work/life balance can be hard to achieve when you can work anywhere at any time. Information can be hard to filter, and pornography and spam take advantage of every crack in the door. Cyber relationships, in 140 characters or less, cannot take the place of genuine, deep, face-to-face relationships.

Let me paraphrase, just for a moment, one of the wisest men who ever lived: "There is a time to connect, and a time to unplug."

* * *

Mary Magdalene was a woman who knew what it meant to have an authentic relationship. We don't know many facts about her life, although there's been much and fantastically embroidered speculation for the last 2,000 years. Only her actions on two occasions are recorded.

The first introduction to Mary Magdalene is in the gospel of Luke, chapter 8. Jesus and a group of followers are traveling the countryside and "proclaiming the good news of the kingdom of God." Here's a description of Jesus' followers:

> The Twelve were with him, and also some women who had been cured of evil spirits and diseases: Mary (called Magdalene) from whom seven demons had come out; Joanna the wife of Cuza, the manager of Herod's household; Susanna; and many others. These women were helping to support them out of their own means *(Luke 8:1-3).*

What stands out most to me in this brief passage is that Mary Magdalene had been demon possessed. While some modern commentators explain away the Bible's mentions of demonic possession as simply mental illness, Scripture is very clear that there is more involved in these cases than illness. Demons or evil spirits are mentioned 63 times in the Gospels alone and were understood as beings who clearly intended to bring serious harm to the people they were inhabiting. Later in the same chapter, a demon-possessed man who lived across the lake from Galilee was likewise delivered by Jesus. If Mary Magdalene's experience was in any way similar, it had been horrific.

This man lived among the tombs in the graveyard outside town. At one time he had been chained and kept under guard, probably to prevent him hurting others. He had superhuman strength, as is often observed in demon possession, and he had broken his chains and escaped. When confronted by Jesus, the demons inside him called themselves "Legion." This was a military term used by the Romans and meant a contingent of about 5,000 soldiers.

So Mary Magdalene had been delivered of seven demons, and her life, which must have been in a shambles, was restored. In gratefulness and recognition of Jesus as her teacher and Lord, Mary left her hometown of Magdala on the western shore of the Sea of Galilee and followed Jesus. We know she was single—because no husband is mentioned—at a time when women were identified as "wife of" or "mother of." This also explains why, instead, she was identified by her hometown, becoming Mary Magdalene as in "from Magdala."

The name "Mary" itself comes from the Hebrew *Miryam*, which probably originated from an Egyptian word meaning "beloved" or "love." It was a very common name at that time, and there are six or seven Marys listed in the New Testament, which accounts for some of the confusion about Mary Magdalene over the years. Mary Magdalene has been confused with Mary, the sister of Martha, and adopted as a symbol of contemplative spirituality. Remember Mary sitting at Jesus' feet? She was also misidentified in the year 591 by Pope Gregory as the sinful woman in Luke 7 who sneaked into a Pharisee's house with an alabaster jar of perfume to anoint Jesus. She wept and kissed his feet, then finished by wiping his feet with her hair. This incorrect identification helps explain why she was often associated with repentance and sexual sin. Neither of these women is the real Mary Magdalene, however.

There's one other notable part of Luke's description of this group of female followers: they supported Jesus financially. They had enough money to leave home and travel independently around the countryside with Jesus and the disciples. One of the women, Joanna, is described as being married to a member of Herod's court, so she may have been quite wealthy. But Luke, a precise and detailed biographer, does not say that she was the sole financial supporter. He describes the women as a group supporting Jesus, so it's likely that Mary Magdalene had financial resources to draw from as well. Her vital role in Jesus' ministry bespeaks a deep commitment to Him.

The next time Mary Magdalene is mentioned is as a front-row participant in the events surrounding Jesus' public execution, His burial, and His resurrection. Her prominent role, detailed in all four of the Gospels, highlights her unwavering devotion to Jesus. Mary Magdalene is named as first in the list of women at the scene of the execution, and John locates her at the foot of the Cross. This strikes me as being both courageous, when the tide of public opinion at Jesus' trial had been so bloodthirsty as to result in a near riot, and heartbreaking as Mary watched her deliverer and dear friend die a slow and agonizing death.

The 12 disciples were nowhere to be found, but the women remained, watching as Jesus' lifeless body was speared and then taken down from the Cross. Mary Magdalene and Mary, Jesus' mother, watched as the body was wrapped in a cloth and laid on a stone shelf in Joseph of Arimathea's tomb. Matthew writes that the two Marys sat opposite the tomb. I'm again struck by Mary's devotion and her faithfulness. At this moment, there's no work to be done and nothing to be gained by sitting outside a sealed tomb with a dead body inside. Why did they stay? They were alone as darkness approached. Perhaps it was simply that their commitment to Jesus went so deep and was so strong that they were reluctant to abandon Him, even when He was no longer there.

Knowing the depth of her devotion, it's no surprise, then, that Mary Magdalene was the first to return, along with some of the other women. Bearing spices to anoint the body, they were stunned to find the tomb open, the body gone, and angels hanging about. Resurrection power was in the air, and the women were not quite sure what was going on. The Gospels describe the women as first afraid, perplexed, and weeping, then progressing to joyful, trembling, and astonished as they began to understand what had just happened.

John provides the most detail about Mary Magdalene's experience at the tomb. First, she saw two angels sitting on the shelf in the tomb. They asked her why she was crying. "They have taken my Lord away," she said, "and I don't know where they have put him" (John 20:13). Mary's devotion transcended death.

Then she heard a voice: "Woman . . . why are you crying? Who is it you are looking for?" (v. 15). I think she was crying hard by this time, unable to look up, the reality of her separation from Jesus finally sinking in.

Perhaps catching a glimpse of a foot or the edge of His robe but not recognizing anyone she knew, she begged for help. "Sir, if you have carried him away, tell me where you have put him, and I will get him" (v. 15).

Then the voice she loved: "Mary" (v. 16). It was the same voice that called seven demons out of her. In shock and surprise, there was a sudden eruption of joy as she recognized Jesus and exclaimed, "'Rabboni!' (which means Teacher)" (v. 16).

By the way, this reunion, with Mary Magdalene surprised by joy, is one of the strongest pieces of evidence that Mary and Jesus' relationship was one of teacher and disciple and nothing more. Although popular books like *The Da Vinci Code* and others have suggested something more intimate, there is no credible evidence to support this theory. The Gospels were written from eyewitness accounts of those who knew Jesus and were participants in the events recorded there, and yet there is never the smallest hint of any type of intimate relationship between the two. This quiet moment between Jesus and Mary Magdalene reveals nothing more than a tender, very committed teacher-student relationship.

The encounter between Mary Magdalene and Jesus ends with his charge to her: go and tell the disciples what she had seen. Ever faithful, she did what He asked: "I have seen the Lord!" (v. 18), she proclaimed.

Mary Magdalene's faithfulness, devotion, and her role in bearing the Good News have inspired countless legends and led Hippolytus, one of the Early Church fathers, to refer to her as "Apostle to the Apostles."

In the end, Mary Magdalene gave up so much; she unplugged from her home, her community, her money, and her time. In return, she found freedom and deliverance, and an authentic relationship with her Lord that transcended death itself.

✳ ✳ ✳

At first I was looking forward to the project I had planned to try to practice the devotion modeled so lovingly by Mary Magdalene. Of the twelve spiritual disciplines listed in *Celebration of Discipline*, the one that came closest to what I wanted to do was practicing silence, or "solitude," as it's called in the book. My idea was to unplug and spend an entire day without speaking, along with devoting myself to prayer and study. "Settle yourself in solitude, and you will come upon Him," said Teresa of Avila.[3]

But I have to admit that my self-interest soon intruded its greedy little head, and as the chosen day drew near, I was rather anticipating some lovely peace and quiet, along with gloating a bit over how easy this project was going to be. But it wasn't as easy as I thought.

Morning broke, and I was still in bed, half asleep. I remembered my solitude project for the day and smiled to myself. My husband was up and about, getting ready for his shower. He saw my eyes open and started chatting. Then he asked "What's on your plate for today?" When I didn't answer, he stopped what he was doing and looked over at me. I smiled. He went on to give me a rundown of plans for his day. Not knowing what else to do, I smiled again, bigger this time. He gave me a funny look, then wheeled around and headed for the shower. *Uh, oh—I better write him a note and let him know what I'm doing, or he'll think I'm mad at him.* I scribbled a note on a scrap piece of paper and shoved it at him when he emerged. "I'm doing a project for my book, and I'm not going to talk today," he read out loud. He laughed and said, "I like it! I can say all the things that bug me, and you can't argue back!" He laughed again.

Hmmm. Not quite the sense of awe I was looking for.

In the shower I wondered if his amused reaction was a harbinger of what I could expect the rest of the day. Maybe it was silly to try to practice an ancient spiritual discipline that was so unfamiliar and, I had to admit, so odd for someone to be practicing today—especially since I wasn't currently living in a monastery.

Downstairs, I was getting started on breakfast when my mom came down the stairs from her mother-in-law apartment and popped her head in the door. "I'm off to the store. Do you need anything?" I just waved and plastered a big smile on my face. It felt so strange not to be able to answer. She paused and stared at me with a quizzical look on her face. "Do you have laryngitis?" I shook my head and showed her my note. Then she did something strange and started whispering. "Well, do you need anything at the store?" she whispered. I shook my head. "Okay—I'm going now," she whispered again.

Next came the kids. My 14-year-old daughter had a friend spending the night, and it was time to wake them up. I went into the bedroom and gently shook them. "Hi, Mom," my daughter said. They both looked up at me with big eyes. I smiled. They looked a little scared. I smiled. They looked even more scared. I showed them the note. They wrote me a note back: "What's for breakfast?" They started to get dressed, moving quickly and talking in hushed voices.

At breakfast my daughter kept looking at me. Every time I caught her eyes, I tried to smile in reassurance. *See? I'm okay. This really isn't that weird—I'm just not talking.* But something about it creeped her out. She hugged me twice, reluctant to let go. Then she wrote me a note asking which woman I was writing about. She never asks me about my writing.

After breakfast, I spent time on my comfy couch praying, reading several Bible passages, and journaling. The late-morning sun was streaming through the window, and I basked in a circle of golden sunlight. I relaxed, enjoying the quiet moment, and then I had an idea for a new writing project. Then more ideas came, then more. I turned to a fresh piece of paper and began to brainstorm, covering the page with ink. All kinds of fresh and creative thoughts were welling up inside of me and pouring out onto the page. It was as if all of the energy I normally used for talking had turned inward. I hadn't expected that.

Later in the morning I did some more reading about the discipline of solitude. I was fascinated by how many times Jesus withdrew to be alone and quiet. There were the famous 40 days in the desert at the beginning of His ministry, but before He chose the disciples, He spent the whole night alone in the hills. (See Luke 6:12.) And when John the Baptist died, He took a boat to a "lonely place." (See Matthew 14:13.) There were five other distinct times when it was recorded that He withdrew to solitude and quietness, and the last and the most well-known was the night He spent in the garden of Gethsemane before He died. If Jesus took care to regularly practice solitude, then perhaps we who follow Him should think more seriously about unplugging from the often hectic pace of life.

At lunch I saw the kids again. I smiled a lot. My daughter hugged me yet again. She looked deep into my eyes. This was highly unusual—she's at the age where she mostly values me as a maternal ATM and taxi driver. I wasn't used to all of this attention from her, but I quite liked it. Just then my son came in the front door from work for his lunch break—his work is just down the street a couple of miles—and I think he intended to test my vow of silence. "Hi, Mom!" he said loud and cheerfully. When I answered with just a smile, he looked at me, eyebrows raised. "That's hard—I couldn't do it," he said. Finally I had earned a little bit of awe.

My mom came down to rustle up some lunch for herself and started peppering me with questions: "Why are you being quiet? Who are you writing about? Is there anything in the Bible about being quiet? What are you going to do next?" I didn't talk but answered a few questions on a piece of paper. It was awkward and slow. Then something new happened. My daughter and my mother began to talk. Recently they hadn't been getting along all that well. They're both a little volatile, and misunderstandings are common. But today they got along beautifully, and I enjoyed just sitting back and listening to them talk. I savored the moment and listened, really listened, and looked at their faces extra hard.

I felt there, but not there.

After lunch my mom got up from the table and kissed me. "I love you," she said. "Living with you is an adventure."

My afternoon was filled with more study, journaling, and prayer. My mind felt alive and alert, and the ideas were still flowing. At dinner it was just my husband and me, and he talked the whole time, relaxed, sharing his day. I just sat back and listened. It was nice to see him unwind, which was often very hard for him to do. Finally my period of silence was just about at its end. Sunset would mark my return to the land of the verbal, and it was about 20 minutes away. He had run out of things to tell me, so we just sat at the table together, companionable in silence, waiting for sunset.

When the clock turned over and I could talk again, it was a relief. But I was a little sorry too. It was a simple thing, really, just keeping silent for a day. But life unplugged gave my husband a good laugh, brought me closer to my daughter, reconciled a grandmother and her granddaughter, prompted my son to appreciate my effort, stirred up my creativity, and led me to savor the beauty of words spoken aloud. But the best gift of all was the chance to set aside time to get to know Jesus better. I plan to do it more often.

HOW YOU CAN HELP CHANGE THE WORLD BY
PRACTICING SOLITUDE

- **Be silent.** Spend one whole day not talking. Be sure to explain to your family what you've planned.
- **Sign up for a silent retreat at a conference center**. Mount Hermon, a Christian Conference Center in the Santa Cruz Mountains of California, is a place that offers guided spiritual retreats. Do some research, and find one near you.
- **Plan your own mini-retreat.** Visit a park, a lake, or a river, and enjoy your own mini-retreat. Be sure to bring your Bible and your journal.

6

SLAG IN YOUR EAR

HOW I WORKED WITH MY HANDS, LIKE ROSIE THE RIVETER

When the war was over, we felt really good about
ourselves. We had saved the world from
an evil that was unspeakable.

—from a letter by wartime worker Laura Briggs

I used to be pretty good at sports. My dad was raised a Texas cowboy and put my sister and me onto horses almost as soon as we could walk. When I was about five, I remember riding Abby, my dad's pretty white Appaloosa mare, and she was so wide I practically had to do the splits to sit on her back. I was a little cocky about my riding skills, and I would wait until my mother, who wasn't so fond of horses, looked over, and that would be my cue. I would dig in my heels and goad Abby into running full-speed down the dirt trail, leaving a dust cloud behind. My mom would pale with fear. I thought it great fun.

Finally, when I was 12 or so I had a full-size quarter horse named Cupid. She was temperamental and unpredictable (typical woman, my father would say), and I had to use all my hard-earned riding skills along with muscle to keep her under control. The horses had to be exercised whether we were in the mood to ride or not, so we rode a lot. The up side was that as a teen I had quite a bit of physical strength and balance from all those years in the saddle—not to mention the years of shoveling horse manure out of the stalls. When it's winter and the manure is mixed with mud, shoveling stalls is much more effective than Pilates or Nautilus, I assure you.

Another strength-building exercise we participated in was slinging around hay bales. We had these big wicked-looking hooks with wooden handles, and with a pair we could hook them into the top of a bale, which weighed between 60 to 100 pounds, and drag it down from a stack in the hay room. Then we used wire cutters to nip the wires holding the bale together, pull the wires out, and fold them up in a bundle. Next we separated a section or two of hay and flung it into the manger for feeding time. As a result, my sister and I were probably as strong or stronger than most boys our age.

My secret strength came in handy one Saturday afternoon when I was 18 years old. I had started dating a college guy named Robert. He and his family were crazy about baseball. When I met him, he played in two leagues: a church league where the guys wore fancy red uniforms and took themselves very seriously, and an informal Saturday league made up mostly of friends. I went and watched him a few times. His favorite position was pitcher, and his grandfather had taught him how to throw a wicked slider. He still curls his fingers into that weird position when he talks about baseball.

A few times we played catch together or did some batting, and he discovered, thanks to my years of horse-wrangling and stall-mucking, that I could hit the ball. Hard.

"Hey—I have an idea," he said one day when we were up on the baseball diamond at the elementary school near my house. "I want you to play baseball with us on Saturday."

"What are you talking about?" I said. "It's all guys!"

Although I knew I could play, I also automatically sensed that a girl wouldn't be welcome in the Saturday guys' league. But I think that's what tickled Robert, the thought that I would shake up their game a bit.

"I want you to play—and hit the ball as hard as you can." Okay, I was starting to get a hint of what he was trying to set up, and I was in.

Saturday came, a gorgeous, warm day. We drove over to Grizzly Stadium in Berkeley, the site for the baseball showdown. It sort of felt as if we were heading to a grudge match, like the big controversial male-female tennis match-up I had heard about back in 1973 that was billed as the "Battle Between the Sexes" with tennis superstar Billie Jean King and little loudmouth challenger Bobby Riggs.

I had a few butterflies in my stomach, and I hoped Robert knew what he was doing. We parked, walked to the field, and instead of sitting on the sidelines as usual, I pulled on my mitt and joined the group. No one said anything at first. The guys just kind of looked at me, then looked away.

"Susy's playing today," said Robert, nice and loud.

A hush ensued. Then the guys adjusted their pants or spit on the ground. I got the feeling they were rolling their eyes inwardly, but with Robert there they remained polite. They picked sides, putting Robert and me together, and our team was out on the field first. I played outfield, and nothing came my way. *Whew! Made it through the first inning without embarrassing myself.* Then our team was up, but I didn't make it up to bat.

The game settled into a rhythm, and I hit a couple of grounders. Then, in the fifth inning, it was showtime. I was up to bat, and as they had in the other innings, as soon as they saw it was me, all the guys moved forward. The pitcher was about halfway between me and the pitcher's mound. The infield guys were not far behind, and the outfield stacked up right behind them. I began to feel the butterflies again. This was it.

I warmed up with a few swings, bringing the bat all the way forward and pausing, pointing it straight out. I looked over at Robert. He smiled. The fielders ignored me, yawning and scratching.

First pitch: a ball. I relaxed, then took another practice swing. Second pitch: I swung pretty hard but hit the ball underneath. Foul ball. Third pitch: I swung hard and hit the ball. Thwack! Right in the sweet spot. It sprouted wings and flew high in the air, way over the heads of every single guy out there. I watched it sailing through the sky, savoring the astonishment on the faces of the opposing team. They just stood and watched it loft over their heads. Two or three guys finally took off after it, but by then I was heading into third base. I picked up speed and ran through home plate. Robert met me at the bag, picked me up in a big hug, and swung me around.

Score one for the girls in that battle of the sexes.

✳ ✳ ✳

The women who headed into the factories and shipyards during World War II were stepping into a man's game, and in many cases they had to weather some pretty foul treatment. When the United States finally abandoned its policy of isolationism and joined the battle to hold Hitler's Germany and To-jo's Japan at bay, the government quickly realized that women were needed to build up production of airplanes and ships.

"We are calling for new plants, and plant conversion to war needs," said President Roosevelt in a radio broadcast Fireside Chat in 1942. "We are seeking more men and more women to run them. We are working longer hours. We are coming to realize that one extra plane or extra tank or extra gun or extra ship completed tomorrow may, in a few months, turn the tide on some distant battlefield; it may make the difference between life and death for some of our own fighting men."[1]

With those highly charged words, the president opened the door to the hiring of millions of women, African Americans, and other minorities who previously wouldn't have been able to get jobs. During the Great Depression, jobs had been scarce, and married women weren't hired because most employers thought one salary should be enough to support any family. In the 1930s before the war, laws and policies were actually in place that prevented the hiring of married women. In addition, many employers had refused to hire women, because the perception was that they didn't have the strength, the mechanical ability, and the emotional stability to do high-paying, skilled factory jobs. But all of that was changing now that America's women were needed.

To persuade women to join the war effort and learn the skills needed to work in the factories, the Office of Wartime Information created alluring promotional campaigns depicting glamorous women in full makeup engaged in all manner of industrial jobs. Eventually they came up with Rosie the Riveter, an image of a woman in safety gear usually portrayed as a welder, as a riveter, or with a jackhammer.

Rosie was most closely associated with a real woman named Rose Will Monroe, born in Kentucky in 1920. She worked as a riveter at an aircraft factory in Michigan. "Rosie the Riveter" was also the title of an original a song by Redd Evans and John Jacob

Loeb, released in 1942. It became a big hit, and the catchy name became a slang term for the women entering the workforce.

In all, more than six million women across the United States left the kitchen or took the children to Mom's and started training for jobs ranging from heavy manual labor in steel mills and on the docks to bus drivers, train conductors, lumberjacks, and barbers. Brute physical strength was not as important as it used to be, because industrial machines now did much of the heavy lifting.

"In less than a year I watched the U.S. transformed from a peaceful country to an enormous manufacturing nation, from having Sunday picnics together to buckling down several days a week to build what was needed for the war," wrote one Rosie named Shirley Hackett. "We all pulled together in a way that I have never seen happen any other time in this country."[2]

But as I experienced out on the baseball diamond, the men in the factories had difficulty adjusting to the influx of women. At times Rosies had to endure rude comments, stares, and catcalls. Women earned a lower rate of pay than the men. They were also watched closely by the male managers to see if they could perform. The women responded.

Most Rosies had never worked for wages before. These "soldiers without guns" usually worked long hours, six days a week. Public transportation was crowded and took extra time. Shopping for groceries was more challenging because of war rationing, and child care was hard to find. But the Rosies were determined to succeed. Edna Hopkins describes her welding training with this story:

> One day my instructor, he comes along and he took my stinger out of my hand and raised up my hood, and the tears were just rolling down, you know, and he says, "Edna, what in the world are you crying for?" I said, "Just look at all these

burns." And he says, "Well, why don't you quit if it bothers you that much" I said, "No, I'm bound and determined that I'm going to do this."[3]

Frankie Cooper took a job as a crane operator in a steel mill. She faced disbelief that she could do the job.

I had to show them I could do it. . . . The women were different in World War II. They didn't want to go back home, and many of them didn't. And if they did go back home, they never forgot, and they told their daughters, "You don't have to be just a homemaker. You can be anything you want to be."[4]

African American women in particular took advantage of the opportunities to move out of deeply prejudiced rural towns and out to the coast to make a new life. A black woman from Oklahoma, Sybil Lewis moved to Los Angeles and went to work riveting airplane parts.

"The war years had a tremendous impact on women. I know myself it was the first time I had a chance to get out of the kitchen and work in industry and make a few bucks. . . . This was the beginning of women feeling that they could do something more."[5]

In the end, the Rosies were a huge asset to the country. *Time* magazine called America's wartime production "a miracle." The Rosies changed the world; who knows—if they had not responded with as much heart and spirit, Hitler's fate and the outcome of the war might have been quite different.

* * *

Although I grew up riding horses and swinging baseball bats, I wasn't as comfortable or familiar with operating machinery. So it was pretty unusual to find myself last week inside a blizzard of burning slag while I operated an arc welder.

It all started with Mike Dorn, a friend of ours who owns a metal fabrication shop in an industrial section of town. It's a small operation, as metal fabricators go, and he does custom work ranging from deck railings outside multi-million-dollar homes to lumber racks and hitches for pickup trucks. Mike let me hang out in the shop for a day, and I spent much of the day looking around at the thousands of hand tools, wrenches, clamps, welding machines, air compressors, grinders, and other materials arranged neatly inside.

"Really, he runs a blacksmith shop," Diane, his wife, told me.

Mike bought the shop from a couple of guys who first really did run a blacksmith shop and then went to work in the massive shipyards that worked overtime during the war. The battered iron anvil that anchored the original blacksmith shop holds a place of honor in the middle of Mike's shop. The guys still use it.

In an amazing coincidence, Mike's mom was named Rose, and when she was a teenager, she and her girlfriend went to work in the local shipyard. Her family, as you can guess, called her "Rosie." So my welding experience took place in the shop of a son of one of the Rosies. It was perfect.

One of the master welders, Alan, explained what I would be doing. "Welding is heating the molecules to between 600 and 700 degrees Fahrenheit. The molecules melt and break down, and you're fusing them back together again." When I watched him work, I could see that the steel melts like butter and becomes liquid. You can then make it flow by how you direct the heat. It turns bright orange red, stays red for a long time, and slowly fades to gray. The heat lasts too.

There are a lot of variables in welding, which is why the human factor is so important. "Machines can't determine how the weather or the atmosphere will affect the steel. There might be impurities in the metal or variations in the measurements," explained Alan. "Computers can aid with a lot of fabricating machines, but any welds that are visible to the human eye need to be done by a person, not a machine."

When the welders in Mike's shop really get cooking, the noise level is outrageous. First, the welding process generates a buzzing and popping noise. There's smoke billowing out, a bluish-gray, thick smoke. Brilliant orange and gold sparks shoot out of the nozzle like a fireworks show. The sparks are burning slag, tiny pieces of molten metal. All the welders have little tiny holes in their pants, shirts, and even in their arms when the odd piece lands and burns through whatever it lands on. "The worst is when you get a piece of slag in your ear," said Alan. "It hurts, and you can hear it sizzling in there, but you can't get it out."

After the weld is finished, it's ugly and bumpy, and the welder has to grind it down. The grinding process creates a high-pitched screech. There's also a constant vibration and rumbling from the air compressors.

After a few hours in the shop, I'm covered in a fine spray of metal shavings. I look at my pants, and they look as if they've been sprinkled with glitter. I see the guys constantly wiping their hands with a dirty rag, and I understand why after I look at my own hands. Welded steel emits carbon, a thin black coating that covers everything in the shop, including the walls.

I wonder about the Rosies and how they coped with the black carbon in the lines of their hands and under their nails. Were they ashamed to have worker's hands? Or were they proud of it, wearing the black as a badge of honor and their participation in the war effort?

When I asked Mike about women welders, he said he hadn't met many. But he did explain that metal fabrication did not require brute strength. Precision is the key, along with spatial and mechanical ability—understanding how things fit together.

Although I was there only a day, and mostly as an observer, I was exhausted when the shift was over. From the constant racket of the machines to the burning metal shooting everywhere to the danger of working around heavy machinery, it was a strain. As the afternoon wore on, the shop began to get warm, and I can only imagine what it must have been like to weld a long shift on a hot day in the factories.

I watched the welders work on, with a slow, measured, steady and careful pace. They worked with finesse, molding and shaping the metal as if it were clay.

After a day in the shop, I'm more grateful than ever to the millions of Rosies who welded and riveted and jack hammered. In my book, they were all homerun hitters.

How You Can Help Change the World by
WORKING WITH YOUR HANDS

- **Swing a hammer.** Lace up your work boots and pound some nails with Habitat for Humanity, an international nonprofit that aims to put a roof over every head. Find your local chapter at <www.habitat.org>.
- **Weave with love.** If you're more comfortable with knitting needles than power tools, get together with crafty friends, and knit lap blankets and shawls for local rest home residents.
- **Go green.** When not on duty at the local shipyard or factory, Rosies worked in their "victory gardens," growing fruit, vegetables, and herbs to aid the war effort by reducing reliance on the public food supply. Follow their lead; keeping a garden is good for you, your family, and the environment.

7

CHICKENS IN THE HOUSE

HOW I HELPED OUTCASTS, LIKE ELIZABETH FRY

Was God really calling her to something that was new?
She was also acutely aware that no woman
had ever done anything so bold.

—Jean Hatton, biographer of Elizabeth Fry

I was about 12 when I saw the chickens in the house.

We had gone to visit my aunt, my father's half sister, in Texas. My father grew up poor in La Grange, a small country town in east Texas. His father, "Big Frank," was a sharecropper, meaning he leased a dusty little piece of land with a tiny house on it, scratched in the dirt, and tried to grow something but never made enough to pay his debts. He took some odd jobs here and there; the longest lasting was at the auction house, where a steady stream of cattle, pigs, and horses were bought and sold. Big Frank was the son of Czechoslovakian immigrants, and he ended up marrying a Czech girl with curly brown hair named Olga. There had been some kind of scandal in Olga's past, and she came into the marriage with a daughter, Pearl.

Frank and Olga had three boys of their own. My dad, Frank Jr., was the oldest, a towhead with brown eyes and an impish grin.

They were the kind of poor that makes visits to the doctor or the dentist out of the question. If you got a toothache, you just hoped it didn't last too long. There were no toys—you played outside in the dirt. There wasn't enough money for food—the kids ate at school as part of a county feeding program.

Then everything fell apart. Olga died suddenly when my dad was ten; no one knew why. Big Frank had some kind of heart trouble and died when my dad was 15. He had to drop out of school and go to work cutting meat to support his brothers. Next, one brother died of a brain hemorrhage. And finally, the youngest died in a brutal car accident, his chest crushed by the steering wheel.

So when my dad turned 18, he had no parents, no brothers, no money, no house, and no education. The only other survivor of the family was his half-sister, Pearl.

My dad just didn't belong in that place, and somehow he had climbed out of the poverty and hopelessness of his childhood. He met my mother, got married, and continued working while he earned his high school diploma in night school. Then he applied to Texas A&M, the prestigious state university.

I marvel now at this now, because no one in the whole family had ever gone to college.

Another challenge: English was his second language. He grew up speaking Czech and didn't learn English until he went to school. But he was determined; he enrolled at A&M, and my parents had a commuter marriage for a while. My mother lived and worked in Houston, about 100 miles away, while my dad went to school. They saw each other on weekends.

When Dad graduated, he got a dream job at Safeway's corporate headquarters in Oakland, California. The young couple packed their few belongings into their Volkswagen Beetle and took off for the West Coast, leaving behind the heartbreak of his early years. They built a new life in California and never looked back.

Until he had us kids. My dad wanted my sister and me to know where he came from. I was 12, my sister 10, and on our trip to Texas we met all kinds of relatives. Most were earning a good living, and several family members had gone on to college since my dad had forged the way.

But not Pearl. She had married a man of some disrepute, a gnarly country boy who liked to hunt, laze around, and drink, and not always in that particular order. They weren't too fastidious in their cooking. My mom recalled a family barbecue in which Pearl's husband served up barbecued squirrel, head and all. My mom watched in horror as Pearl held the squirrel carcass down on the plate, cracked open the head, and ate the brain.

So on this trip my dad decided that we needed to go and visit Aunt Pearl and her brood. We bounced over a dirt road out to their place, an old wooden house surrounded by weeds. At one point the house had been white, but it had shed most of its paint years ago. We climbed some rickety steps, and I pushed my little sister ahead of me onto the porch; I figured if she stepped through a rotten board, I could pull her up easier than she could pull me. The front door was open; Pearl emerged from the dark interior to greet us. She had inherited curly brown hair from her mother. We followed her in and looked around as our eyes adjusted. There was a bed in the middle of the room, so we sat there. When I plopped down, a big cloud of dust billowed up. I was sorry I had worn shorts.

A doorway to our left was covered by a dirty, torn blanket nailed across the doorframe, leaving a two-foot opening at the bottom. A teenage boy with a mullet emerged from the hole. He was holding a large brown piece of something nasty. "Look at

this snake I killed!" he said with a big grin. "I skinned it myself."
It was all raggedy around the edges. He waved it at us. "Want to
touch it?"

My parents' faces looked a little strained. That was just about
the time the chickens walked through the room. I nudged my
sister, and we both stared. They casually walked through, as if
they were on an evening stroll, turning their heads this way and
that, I suppose on the lookout for something to eat. What exactly were they looking for? They were scrawny, feathers askew.
One paused, cocked his head, and stared me down with a beady
black eye. Then he pecked the floor several times, scratching
quickly with one foot. *What was he eating?*

Then something growled outside. A couple of mangy-looking
brown dogs ran through the open front door, chasing each other.
They spotted the chickens, and the chase was on. The chickens
skedaddled into the back of the house, dogs in full pursuit.

I don't remember what happened after that, except that I saw
my dad give Pearl some money. When we left, he looked sad and
didn't say much. I think he had caught a glimpse of a long-ago
life.

Somehow Pearl and her family were stuck. I shuddered, and
I started to understand what it must have been like to grow up in
that dusty, hardscrabble existence.

Poverty scares me. I saw where my dad came from, and I
don't want to go there. It's a place of darkness and ignorance,
hopelessness and pain. It's a place without safety nets, where
everything and everyone you love can be stripped away from you,
as it was for my dad. It's a place where your life has been so hard
that you just don't care anymore, and you just give up and let
your dogs chase chickens through your house.

Most of my life I've avoided having anything to do with people in these kinds of desperate situations. I've tried hard to avoid

seeing people in misery. After all, if I ignore it, I can pretend it doesn't exist. Right? And then it can't happen to me.

* * *

Thankfully for the people suffering in London's notorious Newgate Prison in the 1800s, Elizabeth Fry was a woman not afraid to look misery in the face. Her lifelong efforts led to a revolution in the way prisoners were treated, relieving the misery of untold numbers of men, women, and children both back in her time and into the future.

Elizabeth Gurney Fry was born in 1780 to a successful banker and businessman in Norwich, England. Both parents were Quakers, a Christian denomination also known as the Society of Friends. Elizabeth's mother believed that girls should have the same well-rounded education as boys, so Elizabeth studied all of the major academic subjects with her mother, along with the Bible. She also accompanied her mother on trips to visit the sick and the poor, with her mother emphasizing the concept of duty. "These desultory remarks are designed first to promote my duty to my Maker," her mother wrote in her journal, "secondly, my duty to my husband and children, relations, servants, and poor neighbours."[1]

Her mother died when Elizabeth was 12, and for the rest of her teen years she suffered from intense fears, especially at night. She also battled anxiety, physical illness, and depression. When she was well, Elizabeth enjoyed all of the opportunities for amusement that her well-to-do status allowed, with parties, dances, and fashion. The Gurney family especially stood out among the Plain Friends, a Quaker faction that dresses in dark, simple clothing and covers their heads (think of the Quaker Oats man with the black hat). When she was 17, Elizabeth was invited to a special Quaker meeting featuring William Savery, an evangelist from the United States. Elizabeth went to show off her brand new purple leather boots with bright red laces, but she got more than she bargained for.

Savery was a powerful speaker who urged a return to simplicity and true religion. He warned the gathered Quakers that they had abandoned virtue for "self-centeredness, indifference and greed . . . In Christian England, people thought more of wealth than of their immortal souls." The audience gasped. Savery went on. "Do not turn from the light that is Christ Jesus. . . . That light is salvation." Elizabeth was listening in earnest now. "No lives are so unlovely, nor so unworthy, nor so lost, that they are beyond the reach of the light. And those who turn to it and are saved will carry its message to other lost souls, and bring them, too, to the light."[2]

Elizabeth was overwhelmed at Savery's words. "I think my feelings that night were the most exalted I remember," she later wrote. "Suddenly my mind felt clothed with lights, as with a garment and I felt silenced before God; I cried with the heavenly feeling of humility and repentance."[3] Elizabeth's profound experience that night set her on a new course; she gave up her fashionable clothes and began dressing as a plain Friend, adopted Quaker plain language, using "thee" and "thou." She also abandoned her busy social life. Her family didn't entirely approve of the change. She seemed so much more serious now.

Soon afterward, she visited some distinguished Quaker friends and one evening felt a strong sense of God's presence. "My heart began to feel as silenced before God," she explained. "Without looking at the others, I felt myself under the shadow of his wing."[4]

One of the Quaker women gave a prophecy about Elizabeth: "A light to the blind, speech to the dumb and feet to the lame."[5] Walking home that night, Elizabeth felt that if she were obedient, she would become a minister of Christ. Although this would not have been a possibility in almost every other Christian denomination, Quakers were unique in that female Friends were allowed to enter the ministry.

Over the next decade Elizabeth married Joseph Fry, who was also a Plain Friend, and began her family, eventually totaling 11 children. When she was 30 she became a Quaker minister but was so busy with her children that she wrote in her diary, "I fear that my life is slipping away to little purpose."[6] She continued her efforts to help the poor and the sick, and her children sometimes felt uneasy visiting the slums with their mother.

Around this same time, a new religious enthusiasm was sweeping over England. One of its most powerful spokesmen was William Wilberforce, Parliament member and the leader of the movement to abolish slavery in England. Wilberforce believed "God had called him to convert Britain to a nation based on Biblical principles."[7] The people of England were hungry for meaning and purpose and ripe for societal change.

When Elizabeth was in her early 30s, a visiting American Quaker minister, shocked by what he had seen on a visit to Newgate Prison, shared his experience with Elizabeth. Newgate was England's largest prison, with more than a thousand inmates. It had a reputation for brutality, vice, and disease. The minister was especially appalled by the conditions of the women's section of the prison, where children and even infants suffered along with their mothers. Familiar with Elizabeth's heart for the downtrodden, he persuaded her to go and see for herself. She went the next day.

Armed with large bundles of baby clothes, Elizabeth and a friend approached the prison. It took some persuasion, but Newgate's governor finally let them inside. At first they heard a far-off babble of voices as they walked through the dark halls. They both gagged at the smell of "unwashed bodies, urine and excrement, alcohol and rancid food, sweat, blood and vomit . . . while the noise of hundreds of voices screaming, bellowing, wailing and sobbing, clamoured in the air and beat frantically upon the ears."[8]

Elizabeth's courage wavered, and she broke out in a cold sweat. The guard unlocked the final door to the women's section, and in the dim light she saw "a seething mass of creatures,"[9] women in a nightmarish state, punching and clawing like animals to get a look at the two Quaker women. They were surrounded, the filthy female prisoners looking, touching, and patting. Elizabeth forced herself to stand still, even when she spotted lice crawling in the eyebrows and hair of the women pressed in all around her.

As the women backed up a bit and gave her a chance to look around, Elizabeth saw "sick women lying on a bare stone floor, frozen in the bitter winter weather, on scanty straw rank with urine." The floors were covered with menstrual blood and blood from childbirth. The babies were almost naked and covered in dirt. The two women got to work and clothed the prison babies in new flannel clothes. As they worked, they cuddled the babies and reached out with friendly touches to the mothers. Wrapping each Newgate baby in fresh clothes and delivering fresh straw for the sick took three days. On the last day, Elizabeth and her friend knelt down on the filthy floor and prayed for Newgate. Some of the women prisoners joined them on the floor, and together they wept over the hopelessness of the lives within.

Family responsibilities kept Elizabeth away from Newgate for a while, but within three years she returned and began the first project of what would ultimately be a full-scale reform of the prison system in England.

She started by asking the female prisoners how she could help their children. They asked for a school, so she founded the first prison school in English history with 30 students. The adult inmates quickly began to ask for instruction, too, in reading and sewing. "If only they had such skills, they said, they need never steal or beg, walk the streets, or be dependent on the whims of men again."[10] The incarcerated women needed something to keep them busy and give them hope for a life outside the walls. During the day there was nothing to do but drink, play games, and fight. At night the guards and male prisoners came in, taking advantage of the women sexually.

Elizabeth began to devise a plan for a workshop where the female prisoners could learn a trade and then manufacture useful items that could be sold for a small profit. To support this project, she formed the Assocation for the Improvement of the Female Prisoners in Newgate. Its goal was "to provide for the clothing, the instruction, and the employment of the women; to introduce them to a knowledge of the Holy Scriptures, and to form in them, as much as possible, those habits of order, sobriety and industry, which may render them docile and peaceable whilst in prison, and respectable when they leave it."[1]

Only two weeks after the prison workshop began, a visiting pastor observed an incredible transformation. Rather than the violent chaos and noise he had experienced before, he was met by a courteous, clean female inmate who curtsied, then took him to see a Quaker woman reading to a group of 16 prisoners, each wearing a clean blue apron, busily sewing. He noticed the room was clean and smelled fresh and was surprised when the women rose and curtsied before getting back to their work. "Already, from being like wild beasts, they appear harmless and kind," Elizabeth said. "Surely it is the Lord's doing, and marvelous in our eyes."[12]

Elizabeth's reform efforts didn't end with Newgate Prison. A few years later she was asked to testify on prison conditions at the House of Commons, and she recommended four major areas of reform: (1) religious instruction, which she considered absolutely necessary; (2) separating violent criminals from younger inmates who had committed less serious crimes, as well as separating out the seriously ill and the mentally insane; (3) training the prisoners for income-producing employment; and (4) establishing prisons that were exclusively female, with female guards and inspectors. The lawmakers responded by passing the Prison Reform Act of 1823.

In retrospect, these reforms seem like common sense, but Elizabeth was fighting against a tradition of public and brutal treatment of criminals. England had a long history of public floggings, mutilations, and executions meant to serve as a deterrent to those who were tempted to commit similar crimes themselves. Elizabeth's ideas for education and rehabilitation were revolutionary and began to spread throughout the country. Other jails, prisons, and even public hospitals and workhouses changed from the influence of her work. Later in life, Elizabeth also set up societies to help the poor and the mentally disabled, instituted libraries for coast guards, and started a nurses' training school. She traveled throughout Europe visiting prisons and promoting her ideas. She spoke to large crowds who gathered wherever she went.

All modern prisons and prison rehabilitation programs owe a great debt to Elizabeth Fry, who started a makeover of the world's prisons with a bundle of flannel baby clothes.

✳ ✳ ✳

With my less-than-illustrious history of trying to ignore the poor and downtrodden, I was impressed at Elizabeth Fry's boldness to go into Newgate and see its horrors for herself, to stare down death and destruction, even as lice were crawling in its eyebrows.

I was amazed, too, at her ability to implant her vision for change into women who had given up all hope. Somehow she reignited a hope for the future and a sense of fresh purpose within their hearts.

As I looked back at my life, I realized I hadn't completely ignored the poor. A local homeless ministry goes out to the streets and distributes meals and clothing to homeless people. Once every few months or so I cooked up some ground beef for burritos or contributed big bags of grated cheese or flats of juice boxes for distribution. Every once in a while I would wonder what it's like out on the street or think about who might be eating the meals I was helping to create. I liked being part of a team that feeds hungry people, but I was afraid to actually meet them.

But Elizabeth Fry's courage gave me the boost I needed to finally go out and see for myself where these meals are going and what homeless people are like. I arranged to go out with the team early on a Saturday morning. I awoke, and my first thought as I lay in bed was this: *The people I'm going to meet today don't have a nice warm bed like this.* I felt the same way in the shower *(How do they wash?)* and when I got dressed *(They don't have a closet full of clean clothes)*. For the first time in a long time, I really appreciated my car, too, and thanked God for it as I drove to where I would meet the team

Team leaders Harry and Juliana Orozco, a married couple, have been working with the homeless for several years. Juliana told me about her first night out with the ministry team. She spotted a man and a woman sleeping on a thin piece of cardboard spread out on the sidewalk. "The woman had no shoes, and it was so cold—I just sat in the car and cried," she said.

The Orozcos head out every Saturday morning with 50 steaming hot burritos in hot boxes, along with 50 plastic grocery bags brimming with sandwiches, fruit, energy bars, and water bottles. They also brew a huge pot of coffee and haul that along with sugar, creamer, and orange juice. It's a feast.

Now we just needed the guests. Harry loaded up the food in their Ford Expedition, we prayed, and then we headed over to the distribution site. I was a little nervous, wondering if the homeless carry knives or even guns. *Will there be fights? Will they attack us?* I wasn't sure what to expect.

I held my breath and hopped out for a look around. At first I really couldn't even tell who the homeless people were. Little groups of men and women stood around the park. Most were chatting, looking relaxed. One guy had a paper and was working on a Sudoku. I saw several backpacks and bicycles. Most people looked neat and clean. As we approached, the little groups broke up and slowly converged. Then the greetings began, with smiles everywhere, hugs, and handshakes. Harry and Juliana were laughing and joking with them like old friends.

We got ready to pray, and one guy asked us to pray for two of his friends. We stood in a circle, and Juliana prayed out loud. Then they lined up on their own at the back of the truck. I helped hand out the bags. Each person waited his or her turn, then stepped forward and took the bag. Just about every single person thanked us. I noticed that the younger guys said thanks but wouldn't meet my eyes. They acted uncomfortable, as if they were ashamed to accept food. The older veteran men and women were more relaxed and seemed fine meeting my eyes. I began to relax a little.

One guy looked really young and clean cut. He had a short haircut, nice shorts and polo shirt, and was probably around 20 or so. I wondered what his story was, but he accepted his bag and bolted. Several people had cell phones. I also saw some with gold chain necklaces and bracelets. They had decent-looking shoes, and their clothes looked clean, maybe just a little soiled around the edges if you looked carefully. If I had passed these people on the street, I would never have known they were homeless.

One man looked as if he had just stepped out of an office building, wearing nice casual dress pants and a collared shirt. He carried a small briefcase. "He's a little crazy," said Juliana. Harry told me he carries around some sort of manifesto in his briefcase, and that's he trying to fight the city, which took away his house years ago.

There was an older woman with nicely arranged hair and a cute pair of shoes. She had manicured nails. Juliana said she lived in a van with a man she had started dating who turned out to be a drug addict. Her family was willing to take her in, but she won't leave her boyfriend.

One older man had a warm smile and a dimple in his chin. Juliana said he was a super-smart mechanical engineer but couldn't kick his addiction to alcohol: "One time we brought him to church with us, and a bottle of vodka fell out of his clothes. He knows better."

I asked them about one grizzled guy I had noticed. He had bright blue eyes, but his face was covered in deep wrinkles. He had thick blond hair and a full beard. He was probably in his 40s but looked 70, and it turns out that he lives in a trailer in Harry and Juliana's driveway. They call it "the homeless trailer."

"We take in some of the guys and give them a place to live. We drive them to the county hospital, get them healthy, and help them find work. We have very strict rules. Some of them make it, and some of them don't. But we've had some guys do really well. They get jobs, places of their own, and get back together with their families."

Wow—I was really taken aback. It was one thing to go out and distribute food. It was quite another to have homeless people living in your driveway. I was impressed that Harry and Juliana were offering practical help, a real step up out of the poverty.

I asked where the homeless slept at night, and Harry said under the overpasses or on the hills above the freeway in small encampments. It's hard for them to hold onto things because anything of value gets stolen or lost.

When all the bags were distributed, we hung around for a while, just talking. The sun warmed our backs, and it was almost possible to believe that we were a group of friends, just hanging out together.

But then it was time for us to go. We said our goodbyes and climbed back in the truck. The homeless men and women walked or rode away, back to only-God-knows-where. I was overwhelmed at my look at people who were really not all that different from me. Some of them looked a little rough around the edges, but they were just people needing a fresh infusion of hope and grace.

I'll never ignore them again.

How You Can Help Change the World by
HELPING OUTCASTS

- **Procurement.** Pack up toiletry kits of soap, tooth-brushes, toothpaste, vitamins, hand sanitizer, and tissues. Add a personal note. Deliver to a local shelter.
- **Cook meals.** Most soup kitchens are always on the lookout for someone willing to cook or bake.
- **Reach out.** Take time to greet the homeless. Smile, chat, and be a friend.
- **Buy it hot.** When you see a homeless person begging with a sign, go to the nearest restaurant and order something hot, delicious, and high protein. Drive back and hand deliver it. Don't forget napkins and a drink.

MEETING THE EXTENDED FAMILY

HOW I LEARNED TO RESPECT OTHER CHRISTIANS, LIKE QUEEN ELIZABETH I

There is only one Christ, Jesus, one faith.
All else is a dispute over trifles.
—Elizabeth I

Small churches can be like small towns: friendly on the surface. I grew up in a small Baptist church in Hayward, California, then one of the more conservative parts of the San Francisco Bay Area. Our church was very conservative in both theology and in behavioral rules. Rock music, alcohol, smoking, short-shorts, long hair, and any other worldly behavior or habits were strictly frowned upon. I remember one of the most shocking moments of my life was seeing one of the deacons out back of the church smoking a cigarette. He quickly flicked it away when he saw me, but I couldn't get the image out of my head. It was the first time I had ever seen a Christian smoke. After that, I kept a close eye on him in case he progressed on to wearing '60s hippy clothes and started saying things like "Groovy." Definitely suspect.

In our family, the week revolved around the schedule of the church. I went to church with my family Sunday mornings, first to Sunday School and then to the main worship service. Sunday evenings I went first to church training and then to another all-church worship service; Monday night, visitation; Wednesday night, a potluck dinner and then prayer meeting; and, more often than not, another get-together during the week for a picnic, revival meeting, or special musical presentation.

Services usually included a welcome, announcements, congregational singing, special music. Right after the special music, the pastor would take the pulpit and preach a three-point sermon. Then came the invitation.

The invitation was a brief presentation of the gospel, and an appeal to the congregation to come forward to receive Jesus as Savior and Lord. We usually sang several verses of "I Surrender All" or "Just as I Am" accompanied by the piano and organ. Sometimes we sang the whole song several times as the pastor waited for people to walk down the aisle and meet him at the front. He would bend down and let the person whisper into his ear whether he or she needed prayer, wanted counsel, felt a calling to become a pastor or a missionary, had decided to become a member of our church, or, the biggie, wanted to get saved. When he figured out what was needed, he would wave over a deacon or Sunday School teacher, depending on the age and gender of the person, and the person was taken to the prayer room where the spiritual business was taken care of.

While the person who had come forward was inside, the congregation continued singing, and when the business was finished, the person was led outside and presented to the congregation. The pastor would stand next to the person while he announced the decision that had been made. The congregation would exclaim with "Amen!" and "Praise the Lord!" with big smiles. The service ended with a benediction, and then came the "hand of fellowship," where a receiving line formed at the base of the platform. Whoever had responded to the invitation would stand next to the pastor, and the entire congregation lined up to shake hands one-by-one and extend congratulations and blessings to the new believer.

As I look back on it, as a rather reserved little girl, I can't believe I had the guts to go forward, but I did. One Sunday I felt a tug on my spirit and decided I wanted to ask Jesus to come into my heart and save me from my sins. I had always loved God, but it was starting to dawn on me that I needed to make a public decision to follow Jesus and to be baptized. The invitation and the music were always compelling, and there was often an air of expectancy, a sense that God was at work in people's hearts and that probably someone was going to come forward and make an important spiritual decision. Rarely was there a failed invitation, but it did happen occasionally, even though the music pastor led us through several rounds of a hymn.

So that Sunday it was me. I felt as if an invisible string were pulling me out of the wooden pew and up the aisle, and I didn't care who was looking or what they thought. At the front the pastor took my hand in his big warm one, and I told him I wanted to be saved. In the prayer room with a kindly older woman, I prayed to receive Christ, and after I said "Amen," I felt a tremendous jolt of joy. All that day I felt as if I were walking with super-bouncy shoes, as if I were extra alive and happy. I knew for sure I belonged to Jesus and was part of His family. I can still feel that goofy-happy feeling if I close my eyes and remember that day, joining the kingdom of God while sitting on that hard metal folding chair in that musty prayer room. I came out grinning and stood happily up front and shook hands with everyone, knowing that we were now brothers and sisters. It was a good day.

Later that week, the pastor came to our house to talk to me to make sure I understood the decision I had made. The first time he came, I was too scared to come out and talk, so I hid in the bathroom with the light off until he went away. A few days later, he stopped by again, and this time I found the courage to come out and answer his questions. I remember his asking me why Jesus died on the Cross. I answered, "To save me from my sins." He seemed satisfied and talked to my mother to schedule my baptism.

My baptism went off well, but on another Sunday not long after, a nice middle-aged couple went forward and informed the pastor they wanted to join our church. He was delighted. As the service ended, he announced their decision, noted that they had recently moved and that they had belonged to a Baptist church at their previous location. He added that they would be baptized next Sunday. All good; we lined up and welcomed them and went off to lunch.

In the car on the way to lunch, I suddenly had a thought: the middle-aged couple I had just given the hand of fellowship to was already Baptist and they had belonged to a church in Texas. Why were they going to be baptized again? I had always heard baptism defined as the public profession of faith, and it only needed to be done once. It just didn't make sense. I nursed my question and waited for the right time to ask.

Lunch was usually at The World's Fair, a food court at the local shopping mall. I ordered a small pizza and sat down to eat with my family at a table in the center. Talk turned to the service and the new couple. I waited. Then a quiet moment. "Dad, why are those people going to be baptized again? Haven't they already been baptized?"

"Yes, they have. But to join our church, they have to be baptized again." That was my first introduction to a certain isolationism I experienced growing up. Don't get me wrong; my coming to faith and my growth as a child of God are a direct result of the sermons, teaching, and discipleship I received at the church of my childhood. But I was more and more puzzled by our youth group's refusal to join other youth groups' conferences and camps, and the knowledge that our pastors would never join other denominations' pastors for breakfasts or prayer meetings. It just wasn't done; our pastor participated only in our own denominations' events and organizations—period.

Probably the most confusing event, and the capstone on my confusion, was when I learned that our church practiced—at that time—a "closed Lord's Supper," which meant that one could not take the Lord's Supper with us unless he or she had been baptized in a church of our denomination. So if Billy Graham had walked in the door one Sunday, he would have been welcome to take the Lord's Supper. But his wife, Ruth, who stayed in the church she was raised in? Sorry. Presbyterians not allowed.

* * *

Queen Elizabeth I, the much-loved monarch who ushered in the golden Elizabethan age of England, grew up in a time when the manner in which you took the Lord's Supper was a matter of life and death, perhaps a very painful, tortuous death.

Most people think of her as the popular redheaded Queen of Shakespeare's time, dressed in extravagant gowns. A lively monarch of a powerful country, she was sometimes known as the Virgin Queen or Good Queen Bess. But many people don't know that she was born on a continent racked by religious wars and corruption, with a childhood marked by fire, blood, and imprisonment.

Born in 1533, Elizabeth's father was the infamous and willful King Henry VIII, and her mother was his second wife, Anne Boleyn. Henry yearned for a son, and when Anne could not provide one, even though suffering two miscarriages, she was beheaded. Her little daughter, Elizabeth, was just two and a half at the time. When her parents' marriage was officially annulled by the Archbishop of Canterbury, Elizabeth became legally illegitimate and was banned from any chance of inheritance or succession.

While Henry continued marrying and executing women in his pursuit of a wife who would bear him a son, Elizabeth was mostly forgotten and raised away from the tumultuous goings-on at the royal court. When Elizabeth was 13, the king died, and she was taken in by the king's sixth and final wife who made sure that Elizabeth received an excellent classical education, including history, rhetoric, philosophy, and languages. Fluent in French, Italian, Greek, and Latin, Elizabeth was the best-educated woman of her generation. She loved to learn and read widely, with a heavy emphasis on Christian thought as well as the Bible. Her tutor proudly reported that "her mind has no womanly weakness."[1]

As Elizabeth was growing up, the Spanish Inquisition was raging, with thousands arrested by the Church, tortured in the most gruesome ways, and publicly executed for not properly adhering to the Catholic faith. With Protestants being burned alive for admitting they didn't toe the line in some of the key Catholic doctrines, Elizabeth took note and resolved, if she ever got the chance, to allow more freedom of thought and opinion. When she was older, she reflected on this turbulent time in a written prayer wherein she thanked God for having "from my earliest days kept me back from the deep abysses of natural ignorance and damnable superstition, that I might enjoy the great sun of righteousness which brings with its rays life and salvation, while leaving so many kings, princes and princesses in ignorance under the power of Satan."[2]

Elizabeth became Queen of England when she was 25 years old, after the brief reigns and then deaths of both her brother, Edward VI, and her sister, Mary, a zealous Catholic who wanted to return England to the "true religion." Elizabeth's early reign was a shaky one, with plotters and conspirators working to put a strong Catholic monarch back on the throne of an England divided into Catholics versus Protestants.

One of her first and most important acts was to cajole Parliament into passing the 39 Articles of 1563, a set of laws that established a legal compromise between Roman Catholicism and Protestantism. Queen Elizabeth's refusal "to make windows into men's souls" allowed the English people to have their own religious beliefs and kept Inquisition-type religious trials away from the country. "So long as her subjects showed outward conformity, there was no effort to delve into their innermost beliefs. By the standards of the day, this was remarkably enlightened."[3]

In many other European countries, any theological belief that did not conform to official doctrine was considered heresy, and the Catholic Church viewed heretics as enemies of society. Inquisitors trying to route out heretics commonly used three types of torture to extract the truth about someone's personal spiritual beliefs. The first was the "strappado," in which the victim's arms were tied behind his or her back. A large rope was tied to the wrists and attached to the ceiling. The torturer pulled on the rope until the victim was hanging by the arms. For extra pain, the rope was pulled and jerked violently, usually resulting in lifts and drops that dislocated multiple joints. This torture technique was used by the Nazis at concentration camps during World War II; it was also used on American prisoners of war in Vietnamese camps during the Vietnam War.

Another often-used torture was waterboarding, in which water was poured over a person's face and into his or her nose and mouth, causing suffocation and a drowning sensation. It's been reported that the average person can stand only 14 seconds of this torture before breaking.

The third and probably most frequently used form of torture was the rack, often portrayed in the movies. The victim lay prone on a wooden frame with hands and feet secured at each end. The torturer ratcheted a mechanical device that slowly increased tension on the restraints, resulting in stretching and slow dislocation of the joints. It was said that people nearby could hear loud popping noises made by the victim's snapping cartilage, ligaments, and bones. With that sort of torture of heretics widespread and routine, it's all the more remarkable that Elizabeth was able to keep England from joining in.

Elizabeth didn't want to rule the hearts and spirits of her people through bloodshed and mayhem. She wanted the love and affection of her people. Likewise, she wanted a church that would appeal to both Catholics and Protestants. Most of the population accepted the religious compromise, and her wise leadership probably helped England avoid the religious wars that plagued other European countries, such as France. The Church of England, which she established, remains in place even today. And somehow she was able to balance the goals and aims of her monarchy, the Church, and Parliament to maintain peace and build prosperity over a 45-year reign in a century of "bitter antifeminism."[4] Perhaps it took a woman with the heart and stomach of a king, as Elizabeth described herself.

Although she was the most powerful woman in the world, Elizabeth recognized her need for God, had her own private chapel in most of her palaces, and was said to spend time praying daily. She wrote down prayers that showed she felt that she was God's vessel on earth, directed by His will. She also acknowledged her own faults and shortcomings (she was known for her swearing), asking for God's forgiveness and mercy. Here's an excerpt from one of the most well known:

O Most Glorious King, and Creator of the whole world, to whom all things be subject, both in heaven and earth, and all best Princes most gladly obey. Hear the most humble voice of thy handmaid. . . . How exceeding is thy goodness, and how great mine offences. . . . And above all this, making me (though a weak woman) yet thy instrument, to set forth the glorious Gospel of thy dear Son Christ Jesus. . . . Thus in these last and worst days of the world, when wars and seditions with grievous persecutions have vexed almost all Kings and Countries, round about me, my reign hath been peaceable, and my realm a receptacle to thy afflicted church. . . . Grant me grace to live godly and to govern justly: that so living to please thee, and reigning to serve thee I may ever glorify thee, the Father of all goodness and mercy. To whom with thy dear Son, my only saviour, and the Holy Ghost my Sanctifier, three persons and one God: be all praise, dominion and power, world without end. Amen.

In the end, it was clear that Elizabeth I was a woman who had achieved absolute power but avoided the intoxicating temptation to attempt to control every thought and belief of her subjects. She held to a moderate course, away from religious strife and persecution and leaning instead toward allowing people to choose their own faith. She explained it like this: "There is only one Christ, Jesus, one faith. All else is a dispute over trifles."

* * *

So while the church I grew up in was made up of generally peace-loving people who certainly could never be accused of torturing anyone for heresy, the isolationism of the church meant that I didn't know much about Catholics or Orthodox or even about other Protestants as a child. As I grew up, went to college, and began attending some churches outside that insular world, I realized that there were lots of other Christians who loved the Lord and served Him in other denominations. In fact, it began to dawn on me that there were millions of Christ followers all over the world forming a global kingdom of God, and many of them were of different denominations.

I recently did some research on Protestant denominations and found such a long list that if reproduced here would take up a large portion of the pages of this book. The Oxford World Christian Encyclopedia estimates that there are over 20,000 Christian denominations, and the United Nations puts its estimate at 23,000. Clearly, there are lots and lots of Christians who have not been baptized in just the way I was and who would not have been joining us in the Lord's Supper of my youth.

The attitudes formed in childhood can be hard to overcome. As I began to read more about Queen Elizabeth's life and the religious conflicts raging around her, I hadn't given much thought to my own attitudes about different denominations. Now that began to change. Inspired by Elizabeth's tolerance for other religious practices and beliefs, I decided to set out to find a worship service where I could mix and meet with lots of other Christians from other denominations. I did some research and found an event planned at Grace Cathedral, a huge, beautiful stone church on top of a hill in San Francisco, just across the bay from where I live.

The occasion was a service called "A Prayer for Peace," a vigil to mark the fifth anniversary of the war in Iraq and a time to remember the dead. Members of San Francisco's interfaith community were scheduled to read on the steps of the cathedral the names of all of the United States military dead, with a special lamentation service to follow inside.

The weather that evening was perfect for lamentation: cold, sad, and foggy. The people who gathered on the steps were cold, sad, and gray like the fog; most were above 40. An air of solemnity dampened conversation, and the few children present and one large, black, standard poodle were kept under strict control. The next thing I noticed when I approached the great Cathedral were the shoes on the front steps; that is, shoes with no one in them. Part of an exhibit on the human cost of the war, hundreds of shoes were arranged across the steps and, inside the cathedral, dozens of army boots tagged with names of dead California soldiers were carefully arranged around the stone labyrinth on the floor. It was a sobering sight.

We stood outside, a ragtag bunch of a couple of hundred middle-aged Californians, and watched the solemn procession of robed figures, multicolored banners fluttering in the wind, as they took their places and began reading the names of the dead. Sweet-smelling incense floated up and disappeared into the darkening sky. A hush descended on the crowd, and it seemed as if the fog enfolded us, this group which huddled against the steps, anxious to finish and climb up into the church for warmth and light. We sang a quiet song called "Watch and Pray."

When the names ran out, the group contracted and flowed, a silent stream of people, through the massive doors of the cathedral. I picked up a booklet by the front door; it calls the cathedral "a house of prayer for all people," a reference to God's description of the Temple in Isaiah 56:7, and also Mark 11:17, when Jesus repeated those words after driving the moneychangers from the Temple. It was a very controversial statement to the Jewish leaders and teachers, who immediately began looking for a way to kill Him. That's God's vision for the Church: a house of prayer for all people. It reminds me of the description of the

New Jerusalem in Revelation—the gates to the city are always open. There is no longer a need to close them.

We sat in rows of hard wooden pews, our feet on the stone floor, our eyes drawn upward by the massive columns that climbed up into the dark, vaulted ceiling high above. The colors of the stained glass windows were muted now in the dusk. People whispered and traded quiet smiles. A guy in front of me with a scruffy beard and brown hair had a quote from Gandhi on the back of his shirt: "Be the change you wish to see in the world." A choir hidden out of sight somewhere at the front sang quietly, in harmony, chant-like songs in English and Latin. A priest spoke about war and how it could be battled with love. We did a response reading from Scripture, accompanied by the extinguishing of candles. These words from Scripture were sung: "In the tender compassion of our God the dawn from on high shall break upon us" (Luke 1:78, RSV).

There were no announcements, no invitation, no hand of fellowship. But music and scripture and the Lord's Supper were available for anyone who wanted to take them. A message and prayer were provided. There were lots of different Christians there in that cathedral, that house of prayer for all people. God was there too.

In the Book of Revelation, the choir in heaven sings this to Christ: "You were slain, and with your blood you purchased men for God from every tribe and language and people and nation. You have made them to be a kingdom and priests to serve our God, and they will reign on the earth" (Revelation 5:9-10).

Inside Grace Cathedral that night I got a little taste of what it will be like to worship with a larger kingdom of God—beyond my small and strangled experience. I liked it—and I think it made God smile.

HOW YOU CAN HELP CHANGE THE WORLD BY
RESPECTING OTHER RELIGIONS

- **Read a book:** Try *The Faith Club: A Muslim, A Christian, a Jew—Three Women Search for Understanding*, by Ranya Idliby, Suzanne Oliver, and Priscilla Warner.
- **Get involved in community church events:** My town has organized several "Church of Castro Valley" events. Five or six churches get together and sponsor festivals and outreach events. Suggest it to your church.
- **Visit local churches:** Periodically worship in different Protestant churches around the area. Be refreshed by the different approaches to worship.

9

INK POWER

HOW I WROTE TO CHANGE THE WORLD, LIKE JANE AUSTEN

*I consider everybody as having a right to marry
once in their lives for love, if they can.*

—Jane Austen, in a letter to her sister

I've always been a bookworm. When I was in grade school, my mom would take me to the city library, always kind of an adventure because we had to run the gauntlet of bums sunning themselves on the grass in front of the library. But it was worth it. Pushing through the glass doors was like entering a treasure cave, with the paper, glue, ink, and ideas more precious than any gemstone.

Heading to the kids' section was like going to the all-you-can-eat buffet at a family-style restaurant when you're starving and you're tempted to grab a plate and skip ahead of the slow old lady who's painstakingly trying to pick the best pieces of iceberg lettuce out of the big plastic bowl. In children's fiction, I was just as impatient with the slow book browsers, especially if they hovered around the familiar spots where my favorite authors resided. I would scan the shelves, head tilted to the right to get a better look at the titles, pick a few books, and start two stacks on the table—one for "maybe/not sure/better page through and see if it's worth carrying home," and one for "definite yes-must-reads."

Eventually, my mom was forced to make a special rule for me: one book a day. "That's so you don't sit in your room all summer, reading until you have no friends left."

"She's always got her nose in a book," my father used to say.

"Let's go play four square," my little sister used to beg. "Stop reading!"

But I was ravenous. I still am.

What are we looking for, we bookworms, dictionary readers, know-it-alls, library fine payers, and hoggers of Barnes & Noble overstuffed chairs? Why do we consume book after book, see "Amazon.com" show up every month on our credit card bills, and experience an accelerated heartbeat when chancing upon a Friends of the Library book sale in a nearby town? What on earth are we—am I—searching for?

I think it might be this: Transcendence.

From a Latin word meaning "to climb above or beyond," transcendence is the goal of most every human pursuit and is the same thing that got Adam and Eve, not to mention Lucifer himself, into big trouble. Here's how I learned that books are a passport to transcendence. One summer I was methodically working my way through all of the Walter Farley horse books, starting with the "Black Stallion" series and with plans to move on to the "Island Stallion" series. An engaging writer with killer pacing, Farley played my emotions like a kid with a new video game, enslaving me to each book to the point that I didn't want to put it down even to run to the bathroom. I remember one afternoon, deep into one of the books, when a long, slow scene of horse cruelty took hold of me. A bunch of tough, mean wranglers were trying to break a wild stallion with some very harsh treatment. The book came alive to me; I was there, right with the horse, feeling every rope, blow, whiplash, harsh word, bitter laugh.

As the scene wound down, the stallion was hogtied, trembling, body worn out and spirit broken. The most masochistic and heartless of the cowboys took a heavy glass bottle, filled with water, and smashed it over the top of the horse's head. As the water ran down his face, the tears began to run down mine. I became hysterical and took off running through the house bawling. I confronted my mom and shoved the book in her face. "There— read this," I sobbed, "and you'll see what real cruelty is."

She stared for a moment at the tears running down my face, then softened. "It's just a book, Honey. Put it down and go wash your face."

Just words on a page. But I had inhaled them, and they had skipped across my synapses and serpentined down around my heart and taken hold. They still haven't let go. Even now, I can still feel the power of those words, still ache for that horse, still grieve for his wildness shattered, his spirit trickling away into the dust.

I realized then the power of words. And I learned how to harness that power. But I mostly used it, this weapon, this magic carpet to transcendence, for my own purposes. For good grades or a paycheck. To impress a boss, beguile a friend, or get revenge. One time, working for a newspaper, I wielded my pen to get back at a waitress who had been slow to serve me. A wicked restaurant review, which was great fun to write, destroyed her in print. She called, furious, and threatened to bring her Doberman and set it loose on me in the parking lot of the newspaper where I worked. I thought it was great fun and told the story to everyone I knew. I gleefully quoted Oscar Wilde: "Never argue with anyone who buys ink by the gallon."

Another time, to fill up a nostalgia column I had been assigned to, I dredged up a horrific 40-year-old story of a woman committing suicide, hanging herself on the bathroom door with the belt from her bathrobe. I remember my perverted fascination, wondering about the logistics—*just how would someone do that?* Her five year-old daughter, Mary, had come home after school to discover her mother hanging there, blue-faced, dead. I faithfully reproduced the story for my column, even down to using Mary's real name. It never once dawned on me that Mary was a real person, that she might still be around, and that she might actually have thoughts and feelings. The day the story came out, the receptionist handed me a note when I came back from lunch. I can still see the words. "Mary came in to see you about your story. She's your neighbor."

The office noise receded into the background as I stared in horror at the paper. I began to tremble. *I did have a next-door neighbor named Mary, and she was, let me think, about 45 years old. Could it be her?*

Shamed, I was (finally!) becoming aware of what I had done, just beginning to perceive the extent of my carelessness and cruelty. My neighbor Mary was the little girl, and I had killed her mother for her all over again. Only this time it was public.

It took a bottle smashed over my head, but I finally got it. Words have power, and writers can use them either to destroy or to transcend. I had destroyed; now I wanted to try for transcendence. I wanted to make a difference. I wanted my words to count.

So I needed a mentor. One of my favorite writers was an eccentric poet who had only seven poems published during her lifetime. But her legacy, bequeathed in ink, is now immeasurable. It didn't take an angry waitress with a dog to steer Emily Dickinson toward transcendence; she wrote only from that mystical place: "If I read a book and it makes my whole body so cold no fire can warm me, I know that is poetry. If I feel physically as if the top of my head were taken off, I know that is poetry. These are the only ways I know of."

Another transcendent writer is Annie Dillard, a spiritual seeker who writes fiction, poetry, essays, and more. She won the Pulitzer Prize for *Pilgrim at Tinker Creek* before the age of 30. Although I'll never match her talent, I share her conviction that writing is sacred, a holy mission to translate truth into nouns and verbs. It's a fool's errand, to be sure, and nigh unreachable. But we try. In *Holy the Firm*, Annie tried to explain the call to her writing students:

> How many of you, I asked the people in my class, which of you want to give your lives and be writers? I was trembling from coffee, or cigarettes, or the closeness of faces all around me. . . . All hands rose to the question. And then I tried to tell them what the choice must mean: you can't be anything else. You must go at your life with a broadax. . . . They had no idea what I was saying (I'll do it in the evenings, after skiing, or on the way home from the bank, or after the children are asleep.) They thought I was raving again. It's just as well.

While Emily taught me that transcendent writing requires reach, and Annie that sacrifice will be required, it was Jane Austen who showed me how to write about the big things and that you can wield words and ink and paper like weapons to fight injustice and perhaps even change the world.

Jane Austen is a 233-year-old English novelist who grows more popular and more influential every year. *People* magazine has declared this "a Jane Austen moment," and the *Washington Post* has called her "the new Shakespeare." Her most well-known novels, *Emma, Sense and Sensibility,* and *Pride and Prejudice,* are the source material for countless films, books, and television shows. Her lesser-known works include *Mansfield Park, Persuasion,* and *Northanger Abbey,* along with a couple of incomplete novels. The self-proclaimed "Jane-ites" form Jane Austen societies all over the world and hold conferences and publish papers. Fans play the "Pride and Prejudice" board game, sleep in Jane Austen nightgowns, cook from the Jane Austen cookbook, and even attach Jane Austen license plate covers to their cars. Jane Austen is hip—the cultural references are omnipresent. "We live in a Jane Austen universe," wrote Jennifer Frey in a piece for the *Washington Post*. "All things about young single women are now mercilessly filtered through the Austen lens."

Why are we so fascinated with Jane Austen? Her work was transcendent. She paired universal themes, such as romantic love, courtship, marriage, and friendship, with a razor tongue so keen, so sophisticated, that she deconstructed the dominant customs of her time under the cover of light and entertaining chick lit-type novels. Jane was a subversive, a radical in a Georgian lady's frock.

Born in 1775, she lived for just 41 years as a poor relation, a single woman without money in a society where marriage meant everything. She lived her entire life in her parents' home, sharing a room with her sister, Cassandra. Her brothers, except for one disabled brother named George, pursued successful careers in the clergy, banking, and the navy. But Jane, with nothing much financially to offer a suitor, never married, although she enjoyed a brief innocent flirtation or two. At the mercy of her parents, and later her brother, she was classified a spinster at the age of 27 and began to dress the part. The only surviving portrait, sketched by her sister, shows a young woman with big eyes, a straight-lined mouth set with determination, clad in a simple dress, her hair covered by a ruffly cap with a few curls peeking out and entirely lacking jewelry or any other ornamentation.

Films and books portray this era as glamorous, with women attended to by legions of servants, presiding over gilded homes with elaborate gowns, hair, and jewelry on display in ballrooms and at dinner parties. But while these women were kept in luxury and ease, they had no legal or economic rights; those were surrendered upon marriage to their husbands. "Not that they missed them," writes Joan Klingel Ray, president of the Jane Austen Society of North America, "because prior to their marriage, all their rights were controlled by their fathers. So the rights were never theirs to begin with."

Under the law, a woman could not do things that we now take for granted, such as vote, get a college education, enter a profession, or control her money, property, or children. A husband could even legally, physically, or emotionally abuse his wife, as she was considered to be his property. Women were utterly dependent on men, whether husbands, fathers, or brothers. Even if a wife did have money, whether inherited or given as a dowry or marriage gift, it was usually "entailed," or legally controlled, by the husband. So when Austen crafted that famous first line of *Pride and Prejudice,* "It is a truth universally acknowledged, that a single man in possession of a good fortune must be in want of a wife," there's great irony woven into those words. The real truth, a desperation-tinged truth, is that young women, Austen included, were seeking men of good fortune, because for Georgian women marriage was everything.

So although Jane Austen is considered the great-great-great-grandmother of today's romance novels and chick lit, for her, writing about romance, love, courtship, and marriage meant that she was writing about women's struggles and concerns. "While women's rights were beginning to be discussed openly and somewhat loudly . . . with her usual tact and subtlety, Austen makes herself heard in a quieter yet steadfast way" (Joan Ray). That steadfast way? Her novels.

Jane Austen changed the world for women in the only way she could: through ink and paper. Even then, she published anonymously, as it wasn't considered proper for a woman to have her name on the cover of a novel. Four of her novels were published during her lifetime, and two after her death. She garnered a couple of favorable reviews but made no great splash in the literary world until much, much later. Her observations on the plight of women in her culture were integrated within the only form allowed her—the romance. Within a convincing love story, peopled by authentic characters rounded with flaws, quirks, and virtues, and seasoned with silken razor wit, Austen transcended the genre to send a message about marriage, summarized in a letter to her niece Fanny Knight: "Anything is to be preferred or endured rather than marrying without affection." While at the time marriage was not just a romance, but also a business deal, Austen looked forward to a time when women could marry for love.

One of the characters fans love to hate is the super-serious Mr. Collins, the clergyman suitor for Elizabeth Bennet's affections in *Pride and Prejudice*. When she rejects his marriage proposal, he pays her back with this solemn warning: "In spite of your manifold attractions, it is by no means certain that another offer of marriage may ever be made you. Your portion [dowry] is unhappily so small that it will in all likelihood undo the effects of your loveliness and amiable qualifications."

Marry for love or for money? Jane Austen didn't want women to have to choose, yet culture dictated that they must. "What have wealth and grandeur to do with happiness?" she writes in *Sense and Sensibility*. "Grandeur has but little . . . but wealth has much to do with it." And from *Mansfield Park* the bottom line: "Everything is to be got with money." Austen created a world, in her novels, where her heroines found their soul mates, where small dowries did not prevent good marriages, and where women were smart, lovely, and loveable. Her books have happy endings, and the money situation always works out.

Living among wealthy friends, neighbors, and relatives, Austen was an impoverished outsider always looking in but never giving in. Rather than marry for money and status, she chose to remain single, creating novels ending in happy marriages full of love and respect, the kind that she herself never experienced. Jane Austen changed the world by creating a more just and equitable world for the women who came to life out of the ink from her pen, and by making that fictional world such a winsome and warm place that its themes of unselfish love and mutual respect translate and resonate so well today. What a grand teacher, who doesn't hit you over the head with the lesson!

Jane found something she was angry about and passionately wanted to change, so she wrote about it. If Jane could do it, maybe I could too. I didn't want to write to manipulate people or sell things. I didn't want to use words as weapons to destroy reputations or dredge up painful family tragedies. I wanted to change things and make them better. I wanted to help people and hold up the banner of truth in my work. So like Jane, I got angry. Then I wrote a book.

* * *

It all started with that publishing phenomenon known as *The Da Vinci Code*. Dan Brown wrote this ingeniously entertaining novel, full of fantastically embroidered myths and half truths, and sold more copies than any novel ever has before; there are currently 75 millions copies in print. No one's quite sure of the book's lasting impact. Will he be the Shakespeare of a future generation? Will there be Dan-ites forming Dan Brown societies and publishing scholarly papers? Stop laughing—it could happen, you know.

But not if I have anything to do with it.

I first heard about the novel when I was having coffee with a friend. "I just read this new book called *The Da Vinci Code*," she said. Something in her voice caught me, an intensity, a resolution. She looked at me: "It explained so many things for me."

The two of us had been very close when we were in school, but our paths as adults were far apart. While I had remained in the faith we were both brought up in, she had begun exploring other spiritual beliefs.

Wanting to see exactly what *The Da Vinci Code* explained to my friend, I went home, ordered a copy, and when it arrived I stayed up all night reading it. I think I may have dented the wall, because when I got to page 238 I threw the book as hard as I could: "Almost everything our fathers taught us about Christ is false," said a main character. A few pages later, the hero claims "Every faith in the world is based on fabrication. That is the definition of faith—acceptance of that which we imagine to be true, that which we cannot prove."

I wasn't angry because Dan Brown made up a bunch of stuff and wove it into a very entertaining story—I was angry because somehow, although *The Da Vinci Code* is stocked in the fiction section of the bookstore, my friend believed everything in it was true. So did many others. Polls suggested that about a third of those who read *The Da Vinci Code* believed its claims were true, were based on solid research, and that perhaps Brown was finally revealing key information that had been kept secret by a crafty conspiracy between political and Church leaders.

Many people in the Church viewed the book as an attack on Christianity and were hopping mad. Lots of arguments and heated discussions broke out, and thousands of people made money off the controversy by teaching classes, writing books, producing documentaries, creating Da Vinci Code tours, and selling Code merchandise. But instead of arguing with people or capitalizing on the book's popularity, I tried to follow Jane Austen's lead and start a cultural conversation about something that made me angry.

A writer friend and I began to study and then share what we learned with groups. Speaking led to writing, and a year and a half later, *Fear Not Da Vinci*, a book co-written with Gini Monroe, was published. Written to inspire people to learn more about the deep spiritual questions raised by Dan Brown's book and to encourage people to use the book and the movie as a way to talk about issues of faith, *Fear Not Da Vinci* was a "letter to the world," as Emily Dickinson once described her work. Sending my thoughts and ideas and feelings out beyond my circle of friends and family was a huge risk and very scary. It took lots of courage, persistence, time, and energy. We suffered late nights, bad backs, sleeplessness, painful wrists, controversy, skepticism, loads of anxiety, and much rejection. Can I just say this? Writing to change the world takes lots of work. But it must be done. Michael Simpson wrote, "Culture may provide us the opportunity to touch vast numbers of people, but we must still choose to endure the discipline of craftsmanship to seize the opportunity."

The end result of all of that effort and expense does not lie in my hands. Books, like children, at some point must be released into the wide, cruel world to live their own lives, make their own friends, and do their own work. Books take on a life that transcends ink and paper and glue as thoughts and ideas are translated into the physical realm. A book, even if read by only one other person, changes the world.

But I still wonder, did my book have any impact? A life changed? A truth learned? A question answered? I have no idea. But, like Jane, I got angry, then picked up a pen. And that is enough.

HOW YOU CAN HELP CHANGE THE WORLD BY
WRITING

- **Start a blog**: "Blog," a contraction for "Web log," is an online journal in which you can share your experiences, ideas, and opinions on the Internet. People interested in your blog can subscribe, and it will be delivered straight to their inbox. Anyone can start a blog. It's easy, low-cost, and sometimes even free. Some blogs have thousands of readers!

- **Write a letter or e-mail**: Many people complain, but few take the time to write. If you do, your ideas and suggestions will stand out. Write personal notes to editors of magazines and newspapers; television and radio producers; local, state, and national lawmakers; and others in positions of influence. Politicians maintain that each letter they receive represents 10,000 voters.

- **Create a Web site:** Like blogs, Web sites are easy to create and cost-effective, too. Many Internet providers, such as cable companies, provide free Web sites to their subscribers. Dozens of Web hosting companies offer low-cost Web site building using premade templates.

- **Get published:** Thousands of books and magazine articles are published each year. Why not yours? Just don't expect overnight success. Start by attending a local writers' conference. There you can begin to understand the business, meet industry professionals, take writing workshops, make friends with local working writers, and maybe even discover a local writers' group.

10

START A LITTLE ADVENTURE

YOU DON'T HAVE TO BE WONDER WOMAN . . .

You gain strength, courage, and confidence by every experience in which you really stop to look fear in the face. You are able to say to yourself, "I have lived through this horror. I can take the next thing that comes along." You must do the thing you think you cannot do.

—from *World War II Home Front,* by Gary E. Barr

When I was a girl, I loved watching a television show called *Wonder Woman.* Lynda Carter played an Amazonian superhero who was strong and beautiful. She wore magic bracelets that repelled bullets and twirled a magic golden lasso that she could use to bind the most powerful villain. She ran like the wind yet somehow her lipstick was always a shiny perfect red and her meticulously styled hair in place. And on top of tirelessly vanquishing evil week after week, she was a genuinely nice person.

When I started this journey, I thought somehow that the amazing women of history I wanted to write about would be just like Wonder Woman: a perfect blend of power, beauty, and niceness. They were not.

I believed that the women who changed the world must have been born with superhuman intelligence or endurance. They had not.

I figured that women who could do such great things came out of the womb with such a superior mix of gifts and abilities that there was no stopping them. But it was not true.

What I found was this: the women who changed the world were just like you and me. Real, flawed, flesh-and-blood women, often lacking education, resources, money, and support, fighting against tradition, prejudice, ignorance, and fear. Every single woman I profiled faced significant obstacles but somehow those obstacles brought out something beautiful, strong, and courageous in her soul, something not always evident at first glance, something hidden away and waiting.

Henry David Thoreau told a story about a family in New England with an old kitchen table that had been in the family for 60 years. A farmer had put it together with wood milled from an apple tree. One day, the table began to make a strange noise, sort of a scratching or gnawing sound. Although no one could ever see anything, the noise continued for weeks and weeks. One day the noise stopped. The family was astonished when a small hole opened up in the middle of the table and a beautiful insect emerged, hatched from an egg deposited in the apple tree many decades before. Heat, accidentally applied to just the right spot by a pot hot off the stove, had brought the entombed creature forth, something alive unexpectedly emerging from something quite dead.

The women who changed the world experienced that same kind of calling, with heat and pressure awakening something powerful and beautiful, hatching the courage to act.

And yet, when I started I was intimidated; I found the sum of each woman's lifelong accomplishments to be overwhelming.

Harriet Tubman led hundreds to freedom and helped bring the Civil War to an end. Mother Teresa tended to thousands in her Home for the Dying. Elizabeth Fry made prisons more humane for many thousands in her generation and for generations to come. The Rosies helped win a war.

But none of them planned on changing the world or bettering the lives of untold numbers of people. Instead, each woman got started by noticing just one need. Then she acted to meet that need. Mother Teresa explained it like this: "We can do no great things, only small things with great love."

I found that one small thing done with love, added to another small thing done with love, adds and multiplies and grows exponentially in some kind of crazy, divine arithmetic until a movement to care for the poorest of the poor catches fire and burns in thousands of other hearts besides your own.

Last, each of the amazing women profiled in this book was honest, transparent, vulnerable, and afraid. At the same time, these women who changed the world were bold, passionate, empathetic, and fearless. They were paradoxical, these women, because they were real.

Remember their stories. Let them inspire and encourage you to leave your comfortable couch. Wherever possible, I've let the women of the past speak their own truth in their own words to create, I hope, a brief moment when you were able to enter into a world very different from your own. My hope is that you will take with you the past and understand a little bit better what led these women to make a difference. The women who changed the world were, after all, just "ordinary citizens fueled by faith."[1]

Want to start changing the world? Take heart; you don't need magic bracelets or a golden lasso. For that matter, you don't have to be a Harriet Tubman, either, or an Eleanor Roosevelt or a Jane Austen. To make a difference and change the world, all you have to do is look around and say this: "What can I do that isn't going to get done unless I do it, just because of who I am?"[2]

Then get up off the couch. And start a little adventure.

APPENDIX 1

THE ADVENTURE CONTINUES
WHAT CAN I DO NEXT?

Continue the inspiration and adventure at <www.solongsta-tusquo.com>.

So Long, Status Quo Web site features

- Readers/Discussion guide
- Free e-articles for your newsletter or blog
- Download a free MP-3 recording of the first chapter
- Download a *So Long, SQ* bookmark
- Download a *So Long, SQ* postcard
- Download inspirational *So Long, SQ* mini-signs
- Download an e-card to send to friends
- Sign up for the "Women Who Changed the World" newsletter (monthly)
- Get in on the conversation at the *So Long, SQ* blog
- Take a quiz to see which of the women who changed the world you're most like
- Join the *So Long, SQ* Facebook group
- Browse *So Long, SQ* T-shirts, mugs, tote bags, and greeting cards
- Bring the *So Long, SQ* seminar to your office, community group, book club, or church

Appendix 2

Quick Bios on Women Who Changed the World

JANE AUSTEN

Born: 1775
Died: 1817, at the age of 41
Country: England
Best known for writing six much-loved novels

Jane Austen was one of a family of six boys and two girls born to George Austen, a country clergyman, and his wife, Cassandra. Jane was educated at home with access to her father's large library. Her closest friend was her older sister, Cassandra. Austen began writing in childhood, first comic stories and later a novella, *Lady Susan,* when she was 19. In her early 20s she wrote *Sense and Sensibility* and *Pride and Prejudice,* which was first offered to a publisher in 1799 and immediately rejected. Next she wrote *Northanger Abbey,* but then took a break from writing to move to Bath, an English resort town, with Cassandra and her parents, now retired. During the five years in Bath, Austen began a novel called *The Watsons,* which was never finished. After her father's death, Jane, Cassandra, and their mother moved first to Southampton and then to a cottage in Chawton, where Jane began to write in earnest. She never married. At the age of 35 she published *Sense and Sensibility,* which identified the author as "a Lady." Then followed *Pride and Prejudice; Mansfield Park; Emma;*

and *Persuasion*. Her health began to fail, and she died at the age of 41, probably from Addison's Disease. She was buried in Winchester Cathedral. Most of what we know about her personal life comes from 160 of her surviving letters, as well as memories written by family and friends. Favorites of readers around the world, her novels have never been out of print.

ELIZABETH I

Born: 1533
Died: 1603, at the age of 69
Country: England
Best known for uniting England's Catholics and Protestants and leading her country into a Golden Age

Elizabeth I was born to King Henry VIII and his second wife, Anne Boleyn. Her father, disappointed in his hopes for a male heir, had Boleyn executed when Elizabeth was not yet three. She was declared illegitimate and raised by various stepmothers. A gifted student, Elizabeth was highly educated and fluent in several languages. King Henry died when Elizabeth was still a teen, and her half-brother, Edward VI, took the throne. When he died after a short reign. Elizabeth's half sister, a devout Catholic, became queen. Elizabeth was accused of conspiring to seize the throne, and although she protested her innocence, she was imprisoned in the Tower of London. Later released, she lived apart from court and enjoyed hunting, riding, music, dancing, and pageantry. Queen Mary fell ill and died and Elizabeth, now in the line of succession, became Queen of England at the age of 25. The new queen quickly took action to reestablish the Protestant Church and soothe Catholic-Protestant conflict. Queen Elizabeth never married, although she received legions of proposals, which she encouraged and entertained for political purposes. The love of her life seems to have been a courtier named

Robert Dudley, who she had known since childhood. He had a poor reputation and was at one point accused of murdering his wife. Elizabeth endured numerous conspiracy plots and assassination attempts, including one revolving around her half-sister, Mary Queen of Scots, a Catholic. After Mary's 20-year imprisonment, Elizabeth reluctantly had her beheaded for her involvement. With the execution, the threats from Spain intensified, and Elizabeth led her country to a rousing victory, aided by disastrous weather, against the Spanish Armada, a massive naval fleet intent on invading England. Elizabeth was very popular with her people, and when she died, she left a united country in peace and prosperity.

ELIZABETH FRY

    Born: 1780
    Died: 1845, at the age of 65
    Country: England
    Best known for reforming England's notorious Newgate Prison

Elizabeth Fry was born Elizabeth Gurney at Earlham in Norfolk, England, to a Quaker family. As a teen, after hearing traveling evangelist William Savery, she began efforts to help the poor, the sick, and the prisoners. She married Joseph Fry, also a Quaker, at the age of 20. After being challenged by a minister to visit Newgate Prison, she did so and never forgot the horrors she experienced there. She returned for the next three days with food and baby clothes. The next few years were spent raising the first few of her 11 children and dealing with financial difficulties. She returned to Newgate in 1816 and soon founded a prison school for the children who were imprisoned with their parents, as well as a workshop for women to learn marketable skills for when they were released. She founded the Association for the Improvement of the Female Prisoners, and her ideas influenced prison administration all over Europe. In 1818 she testified to a House of Commons committee on British prison conditions, becoming the first woman to present evidence in Parliament. She also campaigned for better conditions for town jails, public hospitals, mental institutions, and workhouses. For most of her life she suffered from emotional problems but learned how to manage her ups and downs. Although Quakers traditionally do not have funeral services, over a thousand people stood in silence as her body was buried.

MARY MAGDALENE

Born: first century A.D.
Died: Unknown
Country: Born in Magdala, in Galilee. Later lived in Ephesus or Asia Minor
Best known for being the first to person to see the resurrected Christ

Mary Magdalene was a Jewish woman from the town of Magdala on the western shore of the Sea of Galilee, four miles north of Tiberias. The Jewish historian Josephus described Magdala as a city of 40,000, but today it is a sleepy village of a few hundred. When Mary Magdalene first appears in the Gospel accounts, she is listed as one of a group of women who traveled with Jesus and supported Him financially. It also mentions that she was delivered of seven demons. She was most likely single, as a husband is not mentioned. Mary Magdalene was one of the women present at the Crucifixion, burial, and resurrection of Jesus Christ. She was the first person to see and speak to the risen Jesus, and He instructed her to go and tell the disciples what she had seen. Mary obeyed and was dubbed by Hippolytus, an Early Church father, the "apostle to the apostles." Legends say that Mary Magdalene lived afterward in Ephesus, Asia Minor, or France. Over the last 2,000 years, her role in the life of Christ has been celebrated, revered, debated, misunderstood, and sometimes co-opted by a variety of groups fascinated by this woman so devoted to Jesus.

PERPETUA

Born: Unknown
Died: 202 or 203 A.D., at the age of 22
Country: Carthage, Africa
Best known for writing an account of her arrest, trial, and Christian martyrdom at the hands of the Roman Empire

Perpetua was an educated, upper-class Roman woman who lived in a cosmopolitan Roman city in northern Africa called Carthage. Although she lived in a very pagan culture, she converted to Christianity in her early 20s. She was soon arrested, along with five others, and sentenced to be torn apart by beasts in the arena. Nothing is known of her husband, but she did have an infant son at the time of her arrest. In jail, she had three mystical visions, which she recorded in an autobiographical account called *The Passion of Perpetua*. She went to her death with dignity and great joy. Her story is the earliest existing piece of writing by a Christian woman. Perpetua is venerated as a saint by the Roman Catholic Church, the Orthodox Church, and the Anglican Church. In ancient Carthage, a basilica was erected over the tombs of the martyrs, and an ancient inscription bearing Perpetua's name has been discovered inside.

ROSIE THE RIVETER

Born: 1943
Died: 1945
Country: United States

Best known for symbolizing the millions of women who did wartime work in the factories and shipyards during World War II

Rosie the Riveter is now probably best known for the iconic image of a female worker flexing her bicep with the slogan "We Can Do It!" Rosie represents the six million women who took over work in factories and manufacturing plants for American men who left to fight in World War II. "Rosie the Riveter" is the name of a popular song released in 1942. It was also associated with a real woman named Rose Will Monroe, born in Kentucky in 1920. She worked as a riveter at an aircraft factory in Michigan. The United States government used the Rosie the Riveter image to create films and posters to encourage women to go to work to support the war effort. For the first time, married women were encouraged to work outside the home, opening the work force for women. The wages earned both motivated women to continue working and helped boost the economy. However, after the war was over, many of the women were discharged, and their jobs were given back to returning soldiers. In 2000, the Rosie the Riveter/World War II Home Front National Historical Park was opened in Richmond, California, where four Kaiser shipyards had employed thousands of Rosies from around the United States.

ELEANOR ROOSEVELT

Born: 1884

Died: 1962, at the age of 78

Country: United States

Best known for traveling around the world as the eyes and ears of her husband, President Franklin Delano Roosevelt, when he was crippled with polio

Eleanor was born into a wealthy family but was a shy and awkward child made even more so by her parents' unhappy marriage and her father's alcoholism. As a teen, her confidence grew with her successful stint at a French boarding school, and she came back home to the States to marry a distant cousin, Franklin Delano Roosevelt. The marriage produced six children, and for a time Eleanor concentrated on being a wife and mother, although she struggled with a domineering mother-in-law. Their marriage became more business arrangement than love affair after FDR's alleged adulterous relationship with his secretary. Although they led separate but parallel lives, Eleanor always supported FDR's political career, especially after he was paralyzed by polio in 1921. Her encouragement and campaigning helped him win the governorship of New York and later the presidency of the United States. Her causes included the poverty relief, the Red Cross, unemployment relief, women's suffrage, education, financial aid for students, job training, child labor, trade unions, civilian volunteerism during the war, and civil rights. After FDR died in office in 1945, Eleanor became a delegate to the United Nations and was instrumental in drafting the United Nations Universal Declaration of Human Rights. Eleanor was popular with the press and wrote numerous magazine articles, had her own radio show, and wrote an extensive autobiography. At her funeral Adlai Stevenson asked, "What other single human being has touched and transformed the existence of so many?"

MOTHER TERESA

Born: 1910

Died: 1997, at the age of 87

Country: Born in Albania, lived in India

Best known for creating the Missionaries of Charity to feed and care for poor and dying people in India

Mother Teresa was born Agnes Gonxha Bojahiu in the town of Skopje, Macedonia. Raised Roman Catholic, she felt a call to missions when she was 12. She was particularly fascinated with the country of India. At 18 she left home and joined the Sisters of Loreto, which operated missions in India. She trained in Ireland, then traveled to India, where she took her vows. She took her Catholic name from Saint Thérèse de Lisieux, the patron saint of missionaries. From 1931 to 1948 Mother Teresa taught at St. Mary's High School in Calcutta, where the poor lived in slums outside the convent walls. In 1946, while traveling by train for a spiritual retreat, she received a "call within a call" and decided to devote herself to working among the Calcutta poor. She received permission from the church and started with an open-air school for slum children. Later she started her own order, the Missionaries of Charity, to aid in her efforts. Today, there are 5,000 nuns and 450 brothers in the Missionaries of Charity, which today has over 600 missions in 120 countries. Mother Teresa's work among the poor and the dying has expanded to encompass orphanages, leper rehabilitation, vaccination centers, and aid to the blind, disabled, alcoholics and refugees, as well as international disaster relief. Mother Teresa received countless awards and honors, including the Nobel Peace Prize (1979), the Albert Schweitzer International Prize, and the Pope John XXIII Peace Prize. Even in her latter years she kept up a punishing workload. She died in 1997 after several years of declining health. Her life and legacy were not without controversy. She has at different times been criticized by cultural, political, and religious critics, the most vehement being Christopher Hitchens, responsible for a harshly critical book and film. Much has been made of Mother Teresa's "crisis of faith," which came to light when letters she wrote to her confessors and superiors were published after her death.

HARRIET TUBMAN

Born: 1820

Died: 1913, at the age of 93

Country: United States

Best known for leading 300 slaves to freedom along the fabled
Underground Railroad

Probably the most famous of the Underground Railroad "conductors," Harriet Tubman, also known as "Moses," led 300 slaves to freedom over a 10-year period. She was born a slave to Benjamin and Rit Ross and had ten brothers and sisters. Beginning when she was six, Harriet was rented out to local farmers. As a teen, she suffered a serious brain injury while trying to protect another slave. This set the pattern for the rest of her life as she sacrificed her time, talents, and resources to care for others. She also served as an army scout, spy, and nurse during the Civil War, bringing official commendation. Later in life, she became an accomplished public speaker and drew large crowds with her presentations at antislavery meetings. She never had children but was married for a time to John Tubman, a free African-American who lived in the South and married Harriet when she was still enslaved. He declined to follow her to the North, even when she made a special trip to meet him. She was crushed when she found out he had already taken another wife. Harriet rescued her entire family and continued to financially support her aged parents, who lived in Canada. Harriet finished out her life in Auburn, New York, where she opened her doors and took in a number of people who were too weak or ill to support themselves. She never received a paycheck or a pension for her wartime service, although many admirers applied to Congress on her behalf. Frederick Douglass said, "Excepting John Brown—of sacred memory—I know of no one who has willingly encountered more perils and hardships to serve our enslaved people than [Harriet Tubman]." And John Brown, who conferred with "General Tubman" about his plans to raid Harpers Ferry, once said that she was "one of the bravest persons on this continent."

NOTES

Chapter 1

1. Sandra M. Jones, "Overabundance of 'Stuff' Sends Consumers Scrambling to Clean House," *Chicago Tribune,* May 5, 2008. <http://www.chicagotribune.com/business/chi-mon-purging-belongings-may05,0,4559208.story>.

2. M. P. Dunleavey, "The High Price of Too Much Stuff," MSN Money, June 26, 2008. <http://articles.moneycentral.msn.com/SavingandDebt/SaveMoney/TheHigh-PriceOfTooMuchStuff.aspx>.

3. Rick Moranis, "My Days Are Numbered," *New York Times,* November 22, 2006. <http://www.nytimes.com/2006/11/22/opinion/22moranis.html>.

4. Ibid.

5. Anne Schraff, *Harriet Tubman: Moses of the Underground Railroad* (Berkeley Heights, N.J.: Enslow Publishers, 2001), 18.

6. Ibid.

7. Ibid., 35.

8. Ibid., 36.

9. Ibid., 58.

10. Charles L. Blockson, *The Underground Railroad* (New York: Prentice Hall, 1987), 99.

11. Gail Collins, *American's Women (*New York: Harper Collins, 2003), 198.

12. David W. Blight, ed., *Passages to Freedom: The Underground Railroad in History and Memory* (Washington, D.C.: Smithsonian, 2004), 112.

Chapter 2

1. Joseph J. Walsh, ed. *What Would You Die For? Perpetua's Passion* (Baltimore: Loyola College, 2006), 11.

2. Ibid., 16.

3. Ibid., 40.

4. Ibid., 66.

5. Ibid., 70.

6. Ibid., 72.

7. Ibid., 78.

8. This is reminiscent of that wonderful prophecy given to Eve in Gen. 3:15—"I will put enmity between you and the woman, and between your offspring and hers; he will crush your head, and you will strike his heel."

9. Walsh, *What Would You Die For?* 78.

10. Ibid., 89.

11. Ibid., 92.

12. Ibid., 95.

Chapter 3

1. James Grant, "Celebs: Legends in Their Own Minds," USC News, September 5, 2006. <http://www.usc.edu/uscnews/stories/12711.html>.

2. <http://thinkexist.com/quotation/every_woman_should_have_four_pets_in_her_life-a/344858.html>.

3. "Becoming Barbie: Living Dolls", CBS News *48 Hours*, televised August 6, 2004. <http://www.cbsnews.com/stories/2004/07/29/48hours/main632909.shtml>.

4. Desmond Doig, *Mother Teresa: Her People and Her Work* (San Francisco: Harper & Row, 1976), 46.

5. Anne Adams, "Mother Teresa: Compassionate Servant of God," *History's Women,* April 27, 2007. <http://www.historyswomen.com/womenoffaith/MotherTeresa_000.htm>.

6. Ibid.

7. Doig, *Mother Teresa,* 144.

8. Ibid., 54.

9. Ibid., 98.

10. Ibid., 119.

11. Richard J. Foster, *Celebration of Discipline: The Path to Spiritual Growth* (San Francisco: Harper Collins, 1998), 47.

12. Ibid., 56.

Chapter 4

1. Edith P. Mayo, ed., *The Smithsonian Book of the First Ladies* (New York: Henry Holt and Company, 1996), 202.

2. Eleanor Roosevelt, Rodger Streitmatter, and Lorena A. Hickok, *Empty Without You: The Intimate Letters of Eleanor Roosevelt and Lorena Hickok* (New York: Da Capo Press, 2000), 22.

3. Eleanor Roosevelt, *The Autobiography of Eleanor Roosevelt* (New York: Harper and Brothers, 1961), 6.

4. Rachel Toor, *Eleanor Roosevelt: Diplomat and Humanitarian* (New York: Chelsea House, 1989), 31.

5. Ibid., 33.

6. Russell Freedman, *Eleanor Roosevelt: A Life of Discovery* (New York: Clarion, 1993), 97.

7. Ibid., 110.

8. Henry R. Beasley and Holly Cowan Shulman, *The Eleanor Roosevelt Encyclopedia* (Portsmouth, N.H.: Greenwood Publishing Group, 2001), 268.

9. United Nations, "Universal Declaration of Human Rights," <http:///www.un.org/Overview/rights,html>.

10. CNN, "World Leaders Gather to Chart Future of Human Rights," <www.cnn.com>, December 6, 1998. http://www.cnn.com/WORLD/europe/9812/06/human.rights.50/.

11. Freedman, *Eleanor Roosevelt*, 154.
12. Ibid.
13. Ibid., 160.
14. Toor, *Eleanor Roosevelt*, 105.

Chapter 5

1. "Press Room," Facebook, <http://www.new.facebook.com/press/info.php?factsheet>.
2. Tamsen Fadal, "40 Percent of MySpace Users are 35-54," <www.wcbstv.com>, July 17, 2007, <http://wcbstv.com/business/myspace.face-book.pc.2.245881.html>.
3. Richard J. Foster, *Celebration of Discipline* (San Francisco: HarperCollins, 1998), 96.

Chapter 6

1. Gary E. Barr, *World War II: Home Front* (Chicago: Heinemann, 2004), 11.
2. Ibid., 17.
3. Penny Colman, *Rosie the Riveter: Women Working on the Homefront in World War II* (New York: Crown, 1995), 90.
4. Ibid., 25.
5. Ibid., 27.

Chapter 7

1. Jean Hatton, *Betsy: The Dramatic Biography of Prison Reformer Elizabeth Fry* (Oxford: Monarch, 2005), 25.
2. Ibid., 64.
3. Bill Samuel, "Elizabeth Gurney Fry," <http://www.quakerinfo.com/fry.shtml>, Aug. 1, 2001.
4. Hatton, *Betsy*, 90.
5. Ibid.
6. Samuel, "Elizabeth Gurney Fry."
7. Hatton, *Betsy*, 153.
8. Ibid., 161.
9. Ibid., 162.
10. Ibid., 174.
11. Ibid., 177.
12. Ibid., 181.

Chapter 8

1. Ruth Ashby and Deborah Gore Ohrn, ed. *Herstory: Women Who Changed the World* (New York: Viking, 1995), 45.
2. Anne Somerset, *Elizabeth I* (New York: Alfred Knopf, 1991), 10.
3. Ibid., 80.
4. Ashby and Ohrn, *Herstory*, 45.

Chapter 10

1. Buckminster Fuller, quoted in Mary Pipher, *Women Who Changed the World* (New York: Riverhead, 2006), 45.

2. Philip Yancey, *Soul Survivor* (New York: Doubleday, 2001).

FOR FURTHER READING

Jane Austen

Laski, Margharita. *Jane Austen & Her World*. New York: Charles Scribner's Sons, 1975.

Michon, Cathryn and Pamela Norris. *Jane Austen's Little Advice Book*. New York: Harper Collins, 1996.

Myer, Valerie Grosvenor. *Jane Austen: Obstinate Heart*. New York: Arcade, 1997.

Ray, Joan Klingel. *Jane Austen for Dummies*. Hoboken, N.J.: Wiley, 2006.

Shields, Carol. *Jane Austen: A Life*. New York: Viking Penguin, 2001.

Elizabeth I

Somerset, Anne. *Elizabeth I*. New York: Alfred Knopf, 1991.

Weir, Alison. *The Life of Elizabeth I*. New York: Ballantine, 1998.

Elizabeth Fry

Hatton, Jean. *Betsy: The Dramatic Biography of Prison Reformer Elizabeth Fry*. Oxford: Monarch, 2005.

Rose, June. *Elizabeth Fry: A Biography*. London: Quaker Home Service, 1994.

Mary Magdalene

Bellevie, Lesa. *The Complete Idiot's Guide to Mary Magdalene*. New York: Penguin, 2005.

Burstein, Dan, and Arne J. De Keijzer, ed. *Secrets of Mary Magdalene*. New York: CDS Books, 2006.

Welborn, Amy. *De-coding Mary Magdalene: Truth, Legend, and Lies*. Huntington, Ind.: Our Sunday Visitor, 2006.

Perpetua

DC Talk and The Voice of the Martyrs. *Jesus Freaks*. Tulsa, Okla.: Albury, 1999.

Foxe, John. *Foxe's Book of Martyrs: An Edition for the People*. Edited by William Grinton Berry. Greenville, S.C.: Ambassador-Emerald International, 2005.

Walsh, Joseph J. *What Would You Die For? Perpetua's Passion*. Baltimore: Loyola College, 2006.

Eleanor Roosevelt

Freedman, Russell. *Eleanor Roosevelt: A Life of Discovery*. New York: Clarion Books, 1993.

Hoff-Wilson, Joan, and Marjorie Lightman, ed. *Without Precedent: The Life and Career of Eleanor Roosevelt*. Bloomington, Ind.: Indiana University Press, 1984.

Kearney, James R. *Anna Eleanor Roosevelt: The Evolution of a Reformer.* Boston: Houghton Mifflin, 1968.

May, Edith P, ed. *The Smithsonian Book of the First Ladies: Their Lives, Times, and Issues.* New York: Henry Holt, 1996.

Roosevelt, Eleanor. *The Autobiography of Eleanor Roosevelt.* New York: Harper & Brothers, 1961.

Toor, Rachael. *Eleanor Roosevelt: Diplomat and Humanitarian.* New York: Chelsea House, 1989.

Rosie the Riveter

Barr, Gary E. *World War II: Home Front.* Chicago: Heinemann, 2004.

Colman, Penny. *Rosie the Riveter: Women Working on the Home Front in World War II.* New York: Crown, 1995.

Mother Teresa

Doig, Desmond. *Mother Teresa: Her People and Her Work.* New York: Harper & Row, 1976.

Graff, Joan. *Mother Teresa.* New York: Chelsea House, 1988.

Muggeridge, Malcolm. *Something Beautiful for God.* New York: Harper & Row, 1971.

Teresa, Mother. *A Simple Path.* Comp. Lucinda Vardey. New York: Ballantine, 1995.

Harriet Tubman

Blight, David W., ed. *Passages to Freedom: The Underground Railroad in History and Memory.* Washington, D.C.: Smithsonian Books, 2004.

Blockson, Charles L. *The Underground Railroad.* New York: Prentice Hall, 1987.

Bradford, Sara. Harriet Tubman: The Moses of Her People. Secaucus, N.J.: Carol Publishing Group, 1997. Originally published in 1869.

Lowry, Beverly. *Harriet Tubman: Imagining a Life.* New York: Doubleday, 2007.

Schraff, Anne. *Harriet Tubman: Moses of the Underground Railroad.* New Jersey: Enslow, 2001.

Weatherford, Carole Boston. *Moses: When Harriet Tubman Led Her People to Freedom.* Illustrated by Kadir Nelson. New York: Hyperion, 2006.

Women Changing the World

Ashby, Ruth, and Deborah Gore Ohrn, ed. *Herstory: Women Who Changed the World.* New York: Viking, 1995.

Collins, Gail. *America's Women.* New York: Harper Collins, 2003.

Pipher, Mary. *Writing to Change the World.* New York: Penguin, 2006.

Samson, Lisa. *Justice in the Burbs: Being the Hands of Jesus Wherever You Live.* Ada, Mich.: Baker, 2007.

Navigate
the unexpected

With humor and refreshing honesty, author Judi Braddy shares the true north points she learned while living in Alaska and explains how these points have helped her keep her bearings— even through life's most battering storms.

True North
Staying on Course Through Life's Changing Circumstances
Judi Braddy

ISBN: 978-0-8341-2341-0

Available wherever books are sold

BEACON HILL PRESS
OF KANSAS CITY

Bridge the gap to better connections.

Through encouragement and introspection, this practical book helps you connect your spiritual life and your daily interactions with the people you love as God begins to change you from the inside out.

A WOMAN and HER
Relationships
Transforming the
Way We Connect

Rosemary Flaaten

A Woman and Her Relationships
Transforming the Way We Connect
Rosemary Flaaten
ISBN: 978-0-8341-2338-0

Available wherever books are sold

BEACON HILL PRESS
OF KANSAS CITY